long live the Wander Society

1. Do you find yourslf increasingly distracted and unable to focus?

2. Do you feel like technology is taking up too much of your attention and time?

3. Do you remember a time when you were much more present with all your activities?

4. Have you had a sense that there is more to life than what you have been doing but you're not sure how to access this?

5. Do you feel disillusioned by a society that seems entirely focused on monetary gain?

6. Do you have a sense that you are experiencing things secondhand, filtered through various forms of media and entertainment?

7. Have you lost a sense of ownership to the place in which you live?

8. Do you find your quiet talents going unused and unnoticed in a world that values bravado, celebrity, publicity, and money?

If you answered yes to three or more of these questions then the Wander Society can offer a respite. This small anonymous organization is looking for thinkers to conduct research. No experience needed. Membership is completely anonymous. The world is waiting for your gifts!

You have arrived.

Seek the unknown.

The Wanderers are everywhere.

WHAT SINGEST THOU?

WALT WHITMAN

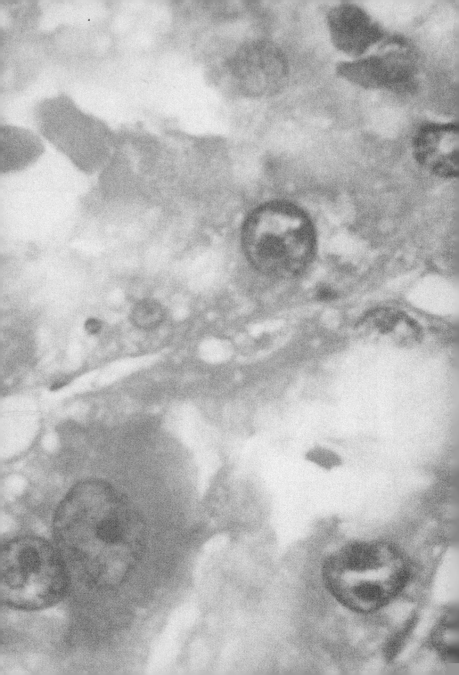

PENGUIN BOOKS

THE WANDER SOCIETY

Keri Smith is a contemporary
artist and the author of the
international bestseller *Wreck
This Journal.* Her work spans a
broad range of media, including
drawing, sculpture, public art,
and book making. She lives in
New England with her family.

THE

WANDER

SOCIETY

Keri Smith

PENGUIN BOOKS

PENGUIN BOOKS
An imprint of Penguin Random House LLC
375 Hudson Street
New York, New York 10014
penguin.com

ISBN 978-0-14-310836-8

Printed in the United States of America
2nd Printing

Set in Chronicle Text G4, Glypha LT Pro, and Metallophile Sp8
Designed by Keri Smith and Sabrina Bowers

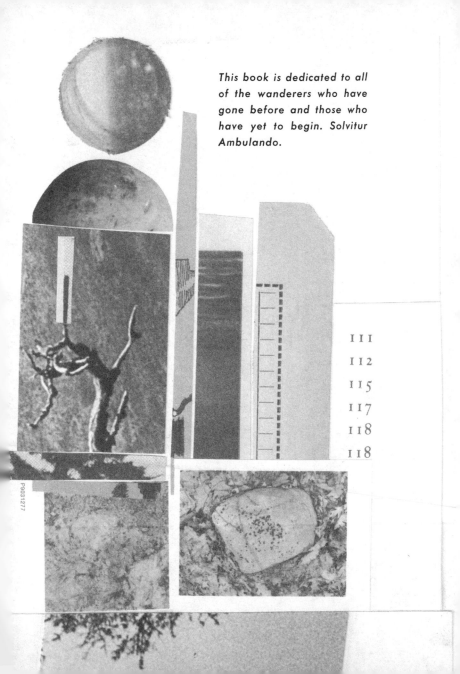

This book is dedicated to all of the wanderers who have gone before and those who have yet to begin. Solvitur Ambulando.

CONTENTS

THE NATURE OF WANDERING

THE WANDER SOCIETY'S TACTICAL GUIDE

WANDERING INITIATION

ASSIGNMENTS/RESEARCH/FIELD WORK

HOW-TO SECTION

INTRODUCTION

Dear Reader,

About two years ago, I was browsing in a favorite dusty old bookshop, one that I frequent when I am in need of a random book find. On this particular day I found myself in the poetry section and picked up a worn hardback copy of *Leaves of Grass* by Walt Whitman. As I began to flip through the pages, I noticed some handwriting in the book. On the inside cover was written "WW will show you the way." On the title page was scribbled *"Solvitur ambulando,"* and underneath that, "The Wander Society" with a small thunderbolt symbol. Fanning through the pages, I found some underlined passages and several more interesting-looking symbols in the margins.

After seeing this I found myself a bit winded and excited. It seemed that this particular volume had its own mystery embedded in its pages. What was the Wander Society? What did the random phrase mean? I wanted to find out more.

I carried the book up to the register and excitedly paid the clerk the fifteen dollars. I left hurriedly, feeling like I had just received a secret message from the universe, determined to find out as much as I could about the Wander Society.

I started with a Google search and uncovered a website for the Wander Society. I hoped it would provide a clue into the group's reason for being. I'll admit: Part of me was prepared to be disappointed, thinking that perhaps this was some kind of promotional campaign for a large uncaring corporation. But when I plugged the URL into the browser, I was greeted with a black page featuring only a white thunderbolt in the middle of the page. Nothing was clickable. Next, I looked up "*Solvitur ambulando.*" The phrase was Latin, and translated to "It is solved by walking." Interesting, but I still wasn't sure what came next. This was clearly going to take a little more detective work—possibly a lot more. But where to go now?

I decided to consult Walt Whitman. He was the source of my discovery after all, and I was intrigued by the message "WW will show you the way."

I should preface the next few paragraphs with the fact that I have limited training in literature. Aside from high school, and both an English literature and poetry class in college, I am basically self-taught. But having worked for upwards of twenty years in bookstores, I do consider myself fairly well read. In my twenties and thirties, I devoured as much classical literature as I could, determined to uncover the keys to existence in the classics of philosophy, Eastern religions, comparative mythology, postmodern theory, cultural theory, and more. In a period that I referred to as "my research," I dove headfirst into works by Socrates, Spinoza, Baudrillard, Benjamin, Barthes, Certeau, Debord, Derrida, Foucault, Eco, Emerson, Husserl, Nietzsche, Sartre, Thoreau, Watts, Steinbeck, Kerouac, Campbell, and Capra just to name a few.

However, despite all of my reading during that time, I am sad to say I never sat down with Whitman. I had read about him in the poetry class and been exposed to a couple of his most popular poems, but the rest of his work somehow eluded my gaze. When I think about it now, his absence during this time seems strange. He definitely frequents a lot of the same circles of literature I was dipping into. But I believe that the right books come to you at a time when you are ready to read them, and I've come to think I wasn't ready for Whitman. Yet.

And so, it is in this way that I came to spend a sun-dappled afternoon on a hammock with *Leaves of Grass*. Only a few other times in my life have I been so moved by a book. Marquez's

Solitude or something
The Wander Society

LEAVES

OF

GRASS

THE "DEATH-BED" EDITION

WALT WHITMAN

Wanderer extraordinaire

THE MODERN LIBRARY

NEW YORK

Love in the Time of Cholera, Kerouac's *The Dharma Bums*, Campbell's *The Hero with a Thousand Faces*, Steinbeck's *The Grapes of Wrath*, and a few others left me with a feeling that my heart had just expanded a couple of sizes. Somehow these books sit in your body and leave it altered in a way that is ineffable. But reading Walt took that experience further.

It was in many ways a physical experience: my chest ached, my breath quickened, and my face flushed. But it was also like the act of reading it was literally causing my soul to open. The best way I can describe first reading Whitman is that it was similar to the sensation of falling in love with someone. You inhabit the world with a giddiness and a joy, as if just existing in the world makes you feel like you are going to explode. (Even now, writing this feels inadequate, the words clichéd.)

Reading Walt Whitman woke up a part of me that wants to run and yell and punch things. It's a feeling similar to when I am working on a creative project and a new idea comes in, and I know I am fully alive and awake and ready to take over the world. I felt like Walt was speaking directly to me in such a close, intimate way, sharing all of his secrets, giving me access to another plane of consciousness, one that I had only scratched the surface of in all of my research.

As I moved through *Leaves of Grass*, I noticed the following passage was underlined:

> *I depart as air, I shake my white locks at the runaway sun,*
> *I effuse my flesh in eddies, and drift it in lacy jags.*
>
> *I bequeath myself to the dirt to grow from the grass I love,*
> *If you want me again look for me under your boot-soles.*
>
> *You will hardly know who I am or what I mean,*
> *But I shall be good health to you nevertheless,*
> *And filter and fibre your blood.*
>
> *Failing to fetch me at first keep encouraged,*
> *Missing me one place search another,*
> *I stop somewhere waiting for you.*

I inhaled deeply, needing to get more air into my lungs.

How was it possible that a book could make me feel this way?

Whoever or whatever this mysterious Wander Society was, it had introduced me to Walt, and I was grateful. I decided I needed to find out more—it was going to be my personal quest. I was unsure exactly what it was or who was at the root of it all. What I did know was that it felt big. So much bigger than me.

I will not lie—I had definite reservations, fears. Most notably a fear of the unknown, something I had felt many times before. And I had no other leads. No next step to take. But I did have Walt, and I knew he had much more to share with me.

The next day, over coffee, I shared my experience with a friend, handing her the book and explaining how it came to me. After perusing it, she looked up at me with a familiar giddy expression, eyes shining.

"What is this?!?" she exclaimed.

"I am not sure," I replied, "but are you in?"

"Definitely, yes."

She wisely suggested I take a closer look at the clues I'd been given. So, later that day, I started a new journal, starting with what I had discovered already:

First up: *Solvitur ambulando. "It is solved by walking."*

Next, the line from Whitman: *If you want me again look for me under your boot-soles.*

Aha! Clearly, I needed to walk, to wander. And so I set out. My only objective was to journey with my eyes open. This was to be my new practice, every day. Open to the unknown, completely awake, I would wander.

A few days later I received an excited voice mail from my friend: "Call me back as soon as possible!" When I got her on the phone she was slightly out of breath.

"What's up?" I asked.

"You are not going to believe what I just found!" she said. "It looks like more from the Wander Society! Can you meet me somewhere?"

We arranged to meet at a local café within the hour.

When I got there, she pulled a folded piece of paper from her pocket. From where I was sitting, I could see "The Wander Society" written on the front, along with the now familiar thunderbolt with the circle around it.

When I unfolded the paper, I immediately saw a photo of a youngish girl wearing a kerchief, approximately fifteen to eighteen years of age, standing on a fallen tree. She had one elbow raised and covering her face as if to hide her identity. In the other hand she carried what appeared to be a small book. There were other photos in the pamphlet all depicting people slightly hidden or on some kind of path.

Interspersed amid the images was the following message:

> An extremely high percentage of great thinkers, writers, philosophers throughout history have been avid wanderers or used the act of walking aimlessly as a way to fuel and influence their work. What is it about the act of wandering that feeds the creative mind? How does it allow us to access deeper layers of consciousness? Wandering is not a mindless task, but instead the opposite, the gateway to enlightenment. A surrender to the great mystery.

The feeling of giddiness came back and I felt consumed by it.

"Where did you find this?"

"It was in a small cardboard station, attached to a telephone pole downtown.

"And that's not all. I also found a sticker with the image of Walt Whitman on a post downtown. We must be living in the center of the Wander Society!"

In the days and weeks that followed, I continued to see references to and imagery of Walt everywhere. Often near bookstores. A couple of times I found the slogans written on walls: "WW will show you the way" and "*Solvitur ambulando.*" Each time, I felt like someone was communicating a secret message just to me. I documented all of them. I confess that I became completely obsessed.

In the meantime, my own wanderings had opened me up in ways that I had not experienced since I was a child. Similar to my experiences with meditation, I still didn't know exactly what I was doing, but it didn't really matter. I felt more present in my body, and I regularly got the urge to run and sing while wandering. What was happening? It felt like I was inside some large interactive game, one that was created by Walt himself. But I still had so many questions.

Over the course of the next year, I collected dozens of pamphlets and pieces of Wander Society literature found in various Wander Society stations all over my town. It is these items that I am sharing with you in this book. During my research I also stumbled onto the website of a professor, J. Tindlebaum. Like me, he had become intrigued by the Wander Society and had made documenting the movements and writings of the group part of his work. It is Professor Tindlebaum who provided me with much more of the literature that I have provided in this book, and I am deeply indebted to him for his generosity and intellect.

It is not my intent to capitalize on the writings of the Wander Society. Instead, I genuinely wish to share its message with you. I can say with all my heart that the practice of wandering has changed my life, and I believe it has the power to change the world if practiced regularly and with an open heart. That is why I am deeply committed to furthering the efforts and endeavors of the Wander Society itself.

While we cannot say for sure exactly who the Wander Society is, I believe its members exist to aid us in our quest to discover our own deepest soul life, to help us move to a higher plane of consciousness. That is the theme that seems to repeat itself again and again in its literature. And it's the message of their undeclared leader, Mr. Whitman himself.

I will end with his own words:

> Re-examine all you have been told at school or church or in any book, dismiss whatever insults your own soul, and your very flesh shall be a great poem and have the richest fluency not only in its words but in the silent lines of its lips and face and between the lashes of your eyes and in every motion and joint of your body.

Sincerely yours,

KERI SMITH

Note: The handwritten comments and annotations are my own personal notes, insights, and observations as I began to document the literature of the Wander Society. What you read is unedited.

FOREWORD

PROFESSOR J. TINDLEBAUM

In January of 2012, I received an anonymous email from someone named "ZenMaster782." The message described an underground organization designed to provide a new way of existing for those disillusioned with current societal constructs by encouraging them to take back control over their mental environment.

As an academic who has spent his thirty-year career as a cultural anthropologist studying self-organizing movements, I was immediately captivated. What was this organization? How did it form?

What I discovered was the Wander Society, a nascent and continually growing group, with its own aesthetics, values, art, literature, and even its own dialectic language. At heart, the group holds a belief in the intrinsic power of wandering as a way to transcend the problems of modern society, access a higher plane of consciousness, and participate in direct experiences of everyday life.

REMINDER TO RESEARCH "ZENMASTER 782." DETERMINE IDENTITY, IF POSSIBLE. UPDATE: NO LEADS ON THIS.

The emergence of such a counterculture in today's society is inevitable. We're facing massive disillusionment with existing political systems, struggling with the overwhelming pressures of modern life, and witnessing the rise of a technology-laden existence. The Wander Society is a backlash, a reclaiming of the power of the individual in a world where choices and freedoms are limited, and almost all of daily life has been commercialized.

Drawing from a long list of writers and philosophers who dedicated themselves to self-examination and believed in the power of free thought to bring individuals to a place of true freedom, the group seems to function as a respite for those who feel powerless and disenfranchised.

HISTORY OF THE WANDER SOCIETY

The earliest recorded existence of the Wander Society dates back to sometime in 2011 (though the exact date of its origins is unknown). At that time, members were recruited through flyers circulated on various college campuses and in urban centers. Today, members seem to be found through email, though it's possible there are other methods I've yet to discover.

> Your ideas are needed! Small anonymous organization is looking for thinkers to conduct research. No experience needed. All interested individuals will be accepted into the organization. Interested parties are invited to view a video for more information. Details will be provided and assignments given. All participation is free. Your imagination is being wasted. Visit thewandersociety.com.

> A sample of the flyer content, circa 2011.

FREE MEMBERSHIP TO

THE WANDER SOCIETY

WHAT IS THE WANDER SOCIETY?

1. Do you find yourself increasingly distracted and unable to focus?

2. Do you feel that technology is taking up too much of your attention?

3. Do you remember a time when you were much more present in all your activities?

4. Do you have a sense that there is more to life but you're not sure how to access it?

5. Do you feel disillusioned by a society that seems entirely focused on monetary gain?

6. Do you feel you are experiencing life secondhand, filtered through various forms of media and entertainment?

7. Have you lost a sense of ownership of the place in which you live?

8. Do you find your quiet talents going unused and unnoticed in a world that values bravado, celebrity, publicity, and money?

9. Do you seek community with like-minded people but often prefer to keep to yourself?

If you answered yes to three or more of these questions, the Wander Society is an anonymous community that can offer a respite. There is no fee to join. The world is waiting for your gifts.

You have arrived. Seek the unknown.

The Wanderers are everywhere.

Whatever the current method, central to all recruitment efforts is a video available on thewandersociety.com.

While the Wander Society seems to resist categorization, and though they are self-described as anti-dogma, this video points to some of the ideas listed in their "Philosophy of Wandering" (see page 11). In the four-minute film and over visuals of random images from nature, an anonymous female narrator talks about how we live in a world "where deep experiences of the world have become diluted or dulled."

The narrator continues:

> [It's possible to] have a much deeper experience of the world through the use of deep looking and regular documentation of everyday life. Through these practices we may be able to create a new narrative for ourselves, one in which we are at the center of a powerful and important adventure. This is who you were when you were very small. This is who you are meant to be.

It is worth noting the similarities of the Wander Society to the Romantic movement of the early 1800s. This should not be surprising given that one of their greatest influences and sources of material is Walt Whitman.

According to the philosopher Isaiah Berlin, the Romantic movement could be defined as "a new and restless spirit, seeking violently to burst through old and cramping forms, a nervous preoccupation with perpetually changing inner states of consciousness, a longing for the unbounded and the indefinable, for perpetual movement and change, an effort to return to the forgotten sources of life."[*] This passage could be describing the Wander Society itself.

---

* Isaiah Berlin, *The Crooked Timber of Humanity: Chapters in the History of Ideas,* edited by Henry Hardy (London: John Murray, 1990), page 92.

THE WANDER SOCIETY TODAY

You probably haven't heard about the Wander Society because its members don't want to be known. But you may have already seen them in your towns and cities, perusing the streets, circling the parks, scavenging in the alleys. If you approach any of them, they will not reveal their identity to you, or readily admit they are a member of the group, so they can conduct their research as quietly as possible. They maintain a solitary existence, preferring to remain anonymous and blend into the surroundings.

Membership doesn't appear to be dependent on any formal acceptance: You are a member if you choose to become one and follow the group's precepts. Members are not required to meet in person, nor does there seem to be any leader or hierarchical structure. They identify themselves to each other using certain phrases transcribed in public places (posters, chalk, and flyers) and through the use of the society's logo: a lightning bolt inside a circle.

While we still do not know exactly who the Wander Society is, we can learn a lot about what they strive for by examining the wide variety of literature they have produced and who their influences are. I have made it my own personal goal to follow the group's progress and document all of my findings. In bringing this information out into a public arena, I am excited to see what new information is discovered by readers in their quest to learn more about the Wander Society.

J. Tindlebaum, PhD, is trained as a cultural anthropologist. He researches and writes on self-organizing communities and digital groups. His first book, *Creating*

Freedom: The Ethics and Aesthetics of Self-Organization, will be published in 2016 by Penguin Books.

Note: The material in this book has been compiled by the author, Keri Smith, from the existing literature found relating to the group. Every attempt has been made to make this guide as complete and as accurate as possible; however, this should be considered, at best, an incomplete picture of the Wander Society. New documents may still exist in some form out in the world. Keep an eye out in case you come across them during your research.

Welcome

You have now become an official member of the Wander Society.

Congratulations! This is not a path chosen by everyone, nor is it a path for everyone. Only unique individuals are drawn to this cause, as it goes against most of what society tells us we need.

Society wants us to live a planned existence, following paths that have been travelled by others. Tried and true. The known, the expected, the controlled, the safe.

The path of the wanderer is not this!

The path of the wanderer is an experiment with the unknown. To be idle, to play, to daydream.

As a wanderer, you are able to see things that others cannot. You've already sensed that below the surface of everyday life - the one that you've been taught to believe in from school, society, family, and whatnot - there's something more interesting, a secret world. You have seen it many times, but now you are ready to access it even more. Most people turn this ability off early in life, but you have let it live.

We are glad you did.

As a member of the Wander Society, you are going to be asked to spend time doing things that are not planned. While participation in the assignments is voluntary, the more energy that is put into the completion of the tasks, the more satisfaction will be experienced. This is true for most things in life.

This is your call to adventure. Shall we see where it will lead?

"Shall I venture to state at this point the most important, the most useful rule of all education? It is not to gain time, but to lose it."
- Jean-Jacques Rousseau, Emile, or On Education

INTRODUCTORY PAMPHLET. FOUND ON BIKEPATH IN NORTHAMPTON, MA.

THE WANDERING PRECEPTS

(A KIND OF MANIFESTO)

1. Wander every day.

2. Do not plan your wanderings. Start in any direction. The location is not important.

3. Use whatever you have. (You have everything you need.) Use your senses.

4. Collect and gather. Document experiences and findings.

5. Remain open. Breathe deeply. Ask the question, "What can I discover?"

6. Allow ideas to come in. Write them down.

7. Question everything you have been told.

8. Use your imagination in your wanderings.

9. Use your intuition. Follow hunches. Go toward what you are drawn to.

10. Encourage your own wild nature. What makes you feel truly alive?

OFFICIALLY BEGAN DAILY WANDERINGS. WHILE I HAVE ALWAYS BEEN A WALKER, MY WANDERINGS USUALLY HAVE SOME KIND OF GOAL OR DESTINATION IN MIND. THE UNPLANNED JOURNEY FEELS MORE DARING THAN I HAD ANTICIPATED.

THE
NATURE
OF
WANDERING

A BRIEF DEFINITION
OF WANDERING

wandering
|ˈwän-d(ə-)riŋ | verb
*the act of unplanned, aimless walking/exploring/
ambling with a complete openness to the unknown.*

Wandering is not about a specific place or destination, getting from one place to another, or movement as a means to an end.
Instead, it's about letting the soul and mind roam.

WANDERING AS METAPHOR

While it is true that wandering often involves walking, it does not always have to. You can also enter into the wandering mindset while sitting. The stationary wanderer can observe, be present, pay attention, and be open to the unknown—all while remaining still. That involves partaking in the wandering rituals, turning off technology, breathing deeply, using the senses, tuning in. For more information, see "Imaginary Wandering" on page 120.

So it is the psychology of wandering that is most important. I can <u>choose</u> to wander whenever I wish. (or enter into the mindset of wandering.)

WHAT WANDERING
IS NOT ABOUT

traveling to distant lands in a literal way,

camping,

moving fast,

pilgrimage,

getting ahead,

material wealth,

religion,

dogma.

THE PHILOSOPHY
OF WANDERING

I only went out for a walk, and finally
concluded to stay out till sundown, for
going out, I found was really going in.

—JOHN MUIR, UNPUBLISHED JOURNALS

Wandering is a state of mind as well as a physical act. You can choose to enter into it whenever necessary. It involves a complete immersion in the current situation, a willingness to be open to whatever comes up, whatever you find in front of you at the moment. It is to exist in a state of naiveté in the truest sense of the word, making no assumptions about what it is you are looking at.

To wander is to enter into a space of existing solely in the present moment. Your only requirement is to observe and have a direct experience with whatever is in front of you (as opposed to secondary or virtual participation).

To wander is to leave behind the complications of living. You can forget the person you are supposed to be for a time, and become who you truly are—unhindered by duties, obligations, and nagging thoughts. To wander is to access your true self.

To wander is to wake up as if from a deep sleep. All of your senses become active and alert again. You breathe deeper. You become curious again. You remember who you were when we were young, before you gave your life to other things (technology, school, money, people).

To wander is to pass through a secret portal to another plane of existence. Time is altered, your mind opens. You're presented with a multitude of magical experiences, experiences meant for you. They are often sensory in nature—sounds, visual happenings, smells, etc.—but occasionally they may come in the form of "signs" that have special meaning for only you: objects dancing on the wind, graffiti that shows something from one of your dreams, a found note, a piece of plastic in your favorite color.

To wander is to connect with all the other wanderers who are bringing their important work to the world. Wanderers are a powerful community. But you may be wondering, what form does a community take that does not meet? Are you not socially isolated by remaining secretive? How can you have a sense of community without meeting?

You connect by partaking in the same activity all over the world, by documenting, by sharing if you choose to. By opening yourself up to unplanned time. By being fully alive yourself.

To wander is to go against the evolution of society. Society wants you to speed up, to produce, to seek material wealth. In a system that requires never-ending growth (at the cost of limited natural resources), to slow down seems anti-progress in nature. Who are you if you are not trying to "get somewhere"? Who are you if you are not actively working toward something? As a wanderer, you're not subject to the narrative forced on you by society. You do not fall prey to trends that have nothing to do with your talents and desires. You do not strive to conform, but instead follow the life that springs from inside. You walk your own path. In this sense, you're truly free.

To wander is to save the world. A world that is dominated by cars, technology, and advertising does not encourage free movement of the body or the soul. It is easy for us to get caught up in this world and its flashiness, but it does not fulfill us on a deep level. Our interest in it is fleeting. Somehow we know this. It is up to wanderers to remake the city into something that ignites the imagination.

> *We save the world by being alive ourselves.*
>
> —*JOSEPH CAMPBELL,*
> **THE HERO WITH A THOUSAND FACES**

We need more rambling, daydreaming, thinking, perusing, being, looking, existing, allowing, ambling, opening, listening, because it teaches us what we are capable of. The nomadic tendency of wandering allows us to take pause, to consider what is really necessary, what is important for living well.

In every moment of wandering, we can experience awakening.

reverie | ˈrevərē | noun
a state of being pleasantly lost in one's thoughts;
a daydream: a knock on the door broke her reverie |
I slipped into reverie.

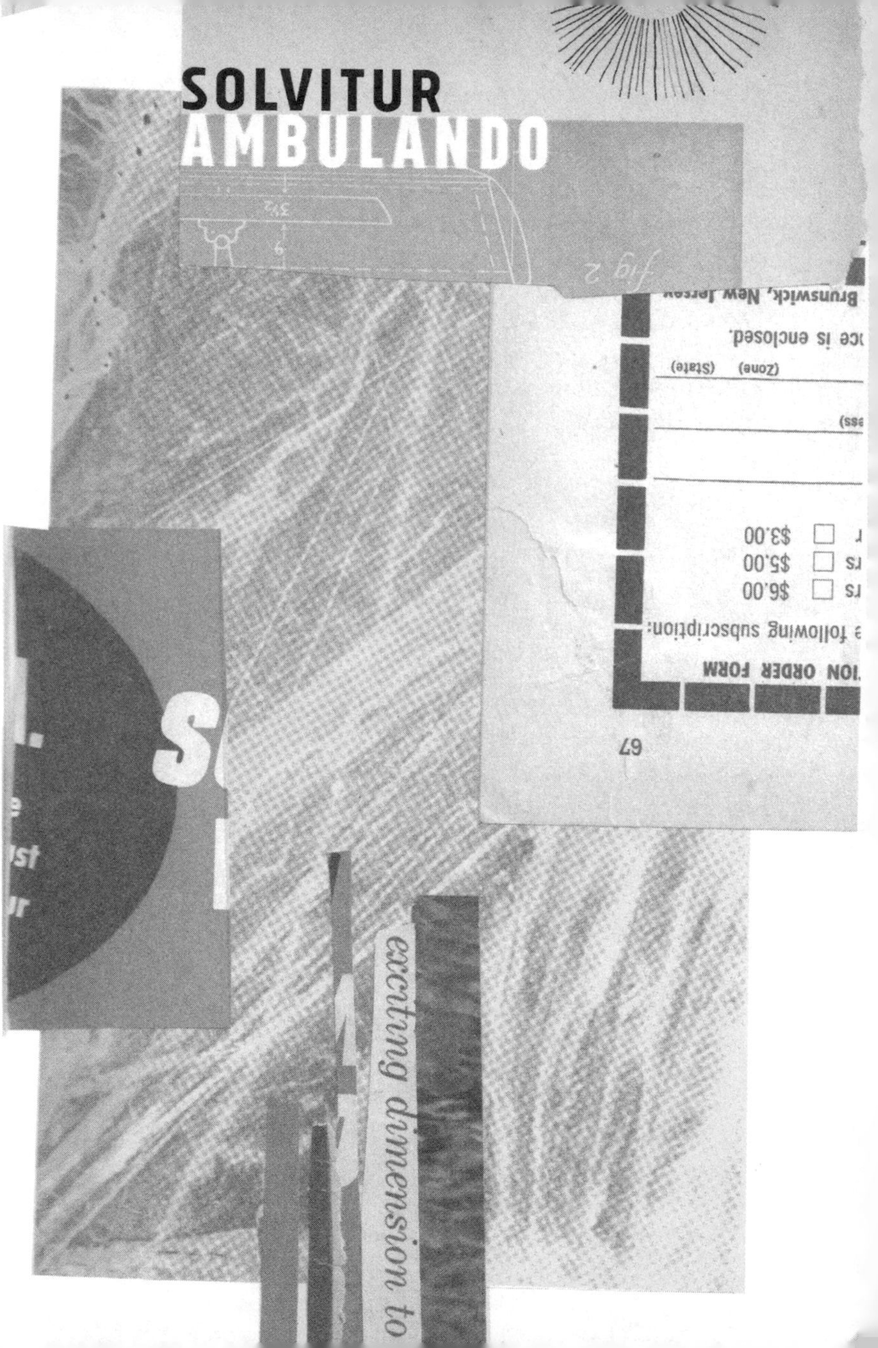

SOLVITUR
AMBULANDO

fig 2

Brunswick, New Jersey

ce is enclosed.

(address)

(Zone)   (State)

r   ☐ $3.00
rs   ☐ $5.00
rs   ☐ $6.00

e following subscription:

TION ORDER FORM

67

exciting dimension to

THE IMPORTANCE OF RANDOMNESS

When we repeat the same activities day in and day out, we limit our ability to have new experiences. Over time our bodies, senses, and brains start to atrophy. Our world becomes smaller and smaller until we are living in a tiny little box.

Society likes us to exist in this box because it makes our behavior predictable. If our behavior is predictable, society is more able to sell us things that we don't need. We tell ourselves that the box is okay, that it is safe, but really the box is a little prison.

How do you know which activities are good for you and which are not? If it is good for you, doing it will give you energy. You will feel charged and powerful, excited, electric, able to take on the world. If it is not good for you, you will feel drained, depleted, lethargic, passive, atrophied.

Deep satisfaction, a sense of fulfillment, new experiences, tangibility, a direct experience of life, connection—these are the things our soul is really seeking. We cannot experience these things by staying in the same little box (literally or metaphorically). We need to push ourselves into new ways of seeing and thinking, alter our course regularly, use all of our senses during our explorations, forget what we know, question things, wake ourselves up.

The wanderer is open to the unknown, to the unexpected, to randomness!

To illustrate this essential openness, we can look at the difference between wanderers and tourists. Tourists make plans and a list of things they want to see, and plot out the day on a schedule. If the plans fall through or do not go the way intended, suffering is the result.

The wanderer does not plan but lets experience tell him or her what will happen, what direction to go in. There are no set criteria to follow. There is no predictability because the path is subject to change at any moment. This openness makes the wanderer much more adaptable and resilient—wanderers are able to enjoy the moment whatever it is. If new experiences present themselves, the wanderer is able to go with the flow.

As wanderers we are not looking for the absence of routine. We are looking to incorporate more spontaneity into our life with the goal of opening ourselves up to the unknown. Life is an experiment. To wander is to seek the unexpected.

Does the act of doing something without purpose challenge you a little?

Good.

> *Milk uncertainty and try to exploit disorder.*
> *—Nassim Taleb, "How Things Gain from Disorder"*
> *(lecture)*

HAVE BEEN HAVING MORE SIGHTINGS OF WS GRAFFITI. TODAY I FOUND A WHEAT PASTE POSTER OF WALT WHITMAN WITH THE LOGO.

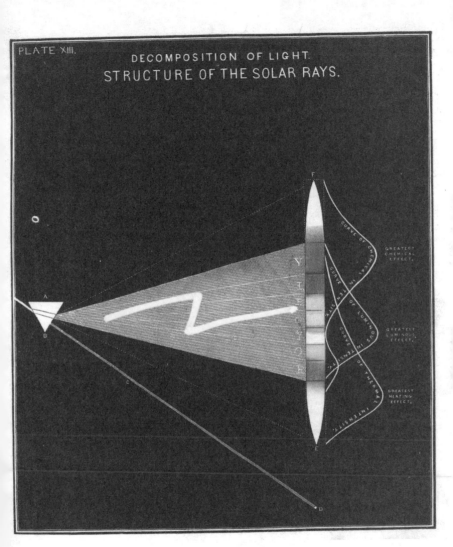

PLATE XIII.

DECOMPOSITION OF LIGHT.
STRUCTURE OF THE SOLAR RAYS.

The beauty of happenstance. Of looking for one thing and finding something else. Of stumbling onto something when you were least expecting it. The book on the shelf next to the one you wanted. Overhearing an interesting conversation. Finding a special sitting spot. In just the right place. Seeing an amazing sunset. Stumbling onto the perfect passage in a book. Discovering a place you want to go for tea. Taking a detour and seeing a different view. A combination of 'happen' and 'circumstance'. To find or come across by chance. Can only happen if we provide the opportunity for them to appear.

FOUND THIS WRITTEN ON A WALL. RAN HOME TO GET MY CAMERA, WHICH I HAD FORGOTTEN.

Sundays @ 6:30 pm at Nirvana Yoga
registration is easy! and required ☺ @ www.na

THE MYSTICAL NATURE
OF WANDERING

Wherever the hero may wander,
whatever he may do, he is ever in the
presence of his own essence—for he has
the perfected eye to see. There is no
separateness.

—JOSEPH CAMPBELL,
THE HERO WITH A THOUSAND FACES

In joining the Wander Society, you are embarking on a hero's quest. The quest is not so much about *where* you wander, but rather your readiness to create your own path, to let go of what society has told you you're supposed to be. When we speak about wandering being a mystical endeavor, what we are referring to is a willingness to confront the mysteries of life: the universe, the unknown. The tool we use to access these places is our own soul. Our soul will guide us to live with our eyes wide open and tuned into what we need, if we give it the space to do so.

The wanderer seeks to discover and participate in that which will give him or her the deepest soul life.

While it may be difficult to explain exactly the concept of "soul life," we all have an awareness of things that cause us to feel more in our bodies, experiences that transcend everyday life.

What is it that moves you? What fascinates you? What makes your heart swell with excitement? What completely absorbs you? What makes you want to run and jump and sing as you did when you were young and free?

WHEN WE BELIEVE IN MYSTERY, WE UNDERSTAND THAT ANYTHING IS POSSIBLE

The act of wandering has the effect of actually altering our consciousness. As you continue your practice of wandering, you will eventually gain more access to this elevated state. You will be able to experience the connectedness of all living things.

The great psychologist Abraham Maslow called these moments "peak experiences." The philosopher William James called this phenomenon "mystical consciousness." The Canadian psychiatrist Richard Maurice Bucke called this "cosmic consciousness." They are all referring to a state of mind that occurs where one feels connected to something greater than oneself. As Bucke describes it in his book *Cosmic Consciousness*, these moments share certain qualities:

> There occurs an intellectual enlightenment or illumination which alone would place the individual on a new plane of existence. . . . To this is added a state of moral exaltation, an indescribable feeling of elevation, elation and joyousness. . . . With these come, what may be called, a sense of immortality, a consciousness of eternal life, not a conviction that he shall have this, but the consciousness that he has it already.

Some things that may happen during peak experiences:

- Complete focus of attention
- Calm, joy, and an absence of fear
- Feeling of being connected to something greater than yourself, of being connected to your surroundings
- Flashes of insight: ideas and solutions flow in
- Alteration of time
- Feelings of deep gratitude for the experience you are having

For this kind of experience, it is helpful that the wanderer continues wandering for an extended period of time alone in a natural setting, usually a minimum of one hour, but preferably longer than this.

When you begin wandering it helps to say to yourself, "I am completely open to a new experience." As time passes, you can start to feel ideas and senses coming to the surface. You will know when it happens because it is often accompanied by an "electric" feeling, as if your molecules are vibrating at a higher frequency. It might make you feel like running or yelling.

Don't worry if you do not experience this at first; it takes practice. The more you wander the more you open yourself up to this energy. The practice of wandering must be continued on a daily basis if possible in order to access this level of awareness.

I HAVE BEEN EXPERIENCING THIS FEELING ON MY WANDERINGS. IT IS COMBINED WITH A DISTINCT "HEART OPENING" SENSATION. I FIND ENJOYMENT IN THE SIMPLEST OF THINGS: CRACKS IN PAVEMENT, LEAVES FLOATING, EARTHY SMELLS — ALL DELIGHT ME. IT DOES NOT HAPPEN ON EVERY EXCURSION, BUT I BELIEVE IT IS BECOMING MORE FREQUENT. WHAT IS HAPPENING? I HOPE IT CONTINUES.

THE MYSTICISM OF WALT WHITMAN

It has been said that Walt Whitman operated on a different plane of consciousness than ordinary people, and that this was apparent in his everyday life and how he approached the world. Psychiatrist Richard Maurice Bucke noted in *Cosmic Consciousness* that:

> [Whitman's] favorite occupation seemed to be strolling or sauntering about outdoors by himself, looking at the grass, the trees, the flowers, the vistas of light, the varying aspects of the sky, and listening to the birds, the crickets, the tree-frogs, the wind in the trees, and all the hundreds of natural sounds. It was evident that these things gave him a feeling of pleasure far beyond what they give to ordinary people.

Bucke also wrote that Whitman was known to deeply affect and permanently alter the lives of many people who spent time in his presence, simply by being with him. He describes the profound effect Whitman had on a man who had met him only briefly:

MAYBE THIS IS WHAT I WAS SENSING WHEN I READ LEAVES OF GRASS FOR THE FIRST TIME? IS IT POSSIBLE THAT THIS ENERGY IS ENCAPSULATED OR TRANSLATED INTO HIS BOOKS? IT MUST BE. WHAT OTHER EXPLANATION COULD THERE BE? IT GIVES ONE THE FEELING OF HAVING AN INTIMATE, PRIVATE CONVERSATION IN WHICH YOU'RE BEING GIVEN SOME VERY IMPORTANT INFORMATION THAT ONLY YOU WILL UNDERSTAND.

He did not realize anything peculiar while with him, but shortly after leaving a state of mental exaltation set in, which he could only describe by comparing to slight intoxication by champagne, or to falling in love, and this exaltation, he said, lasted at least six weeks in a clearly marked degree, so that, for at least that length of time, he was plainly different from his ordinary self.

This effect was also known to occur with small children who reputedly would flock to him and very often become so comfortable and soothed they would fall asleep on his lap.

It is this state of being absolutely tuned into the present moment, and of complete immersion in the natural world that we, the members of the Wander Society, aspire to. It is for this reason that we look to the work and the life of Walt Whitman, as he serves as a beacon and role model for our community.

USE YOUR POWERS

Using intuition is another method of accessing a higher level of consciousness. These powers exist in you right now at all times. Sometimes you just need to tune into them in order to hear their messages. You can find answers to all kinds of issues, such as *What direction should I head in? What path should I take? What gives me energy? Who gives me energy? What should I spend my time doing? How can I contribute to the world?*

Some Clues to Help Guide You

Tune into how your intuition communicates with you. Do you feel things in your body? Do you get a visual image? Do you receive new thoughts?

Listen. Find quiet using meditation or wandering. Turn off technology.

Write. Begin by writing stream of consciousness, whatever comes into your mind. Do not censor yourself. See if anything interesting comes up.

Ask your intuition to speak to you. Verbalize that you are now open to receiving messages in a way that you can easily understand.

Think of yourself as a large vibrating ball of energy, which you are. The more in touch with your powers that you are, the more light you radiate, the more you will attract people, situations, and opportunities to you. When we get in touch with our powers, we are actually living the life we are meant to, one that is in tune with what will fulfill us, as opposed to one that society has told us we should live.

Our intuition will often give us messages that are counter to societal mores. Your spirit might long to take a naked swim in a pond on a hot day. These longings will feel crazy and intense. You will feel a bit giddy and anxious.

The more we follow our intuitive urges, the more we are inhabiting the life we are meant to lead, the life that will fulfill our innermost desires.

The wanderer becomes one with himself or herself and the universe. We connect with the energy of all living things. We live according to our inner nature.

I HAVE BEEN EXPERIENCING THIS SENSATION (GLOWING)! DID A WANDER THIS MORNING AND FELT THE URGE TO RUN. THIS EXPANDED CONSCIOUSNESS IS BECOMING MORE FREQUENT.

> *The soul of the world had opened and I fantasized that everything wicked, distressing and painful was on the point of vanishing. . . . All notion of the future paled and the past dissolved. In the glowing present, I myself glowed.*

—ROBERT WALSER, THE WALK

One must create and participate in a variety of rituals designed to communicate to the psyche that we are now going to change gears and enter into our wandering mindset, and that the manner in which we have been operating is now about to undergo a drastic change. These rituals include a gathering of tools, a wearing of a wandering uniform, a reciting/reading of the Wander's Manifesto, and summoning the spirits of fellow wanderers.

When we enter into the wandering mindset, which can take a while to kick in, we actually change into our true self, not the person we are trying to be for society. This is the nature of this quest. Our mind takes a journey and through it we learn to trust ourselves.

> *A pleasant walk most often veritably teems with imageries, living poems, attractive objects, natural beauties, be they ever so small. The lore of nature and the lore of the country are revealed, charming and graceful, to the sense and eyes of the observant walker, who must of course walk not with downcast but with open and unclouded eyes.*

—ROBERT WALSER, THE WALK

Wandering is extremely powerful. Use this power wisely. Do not speak of this power with others unless they are able to hear it. Some people are not open to these kinds of ideas. Never mind them. You have your own work to do.

Do not be concerned with the work of others or comparing yourself to others. Everyone is on their own path. Comparing one

path to another is a useless endeavor; it does not take into account the incredible complexity of each individual's life experience, what we are each here to learn, what we are each here to do.

The Wander Society treats each individual as its own unique force, full of beauty and mystery, and wielding immense power. In becoming a member of the Wander Society, we accept and acknowledge our own incredible power.

THE WANDER SOCIETY

WE ARE INFINITE

THE WANDER SOCIETY

What we really long for, what we have always wanted is to be deeply connected.

THE WANDER SOCIETY

Wander Society Mini Zines
found in various locations

search for healing

This is what
you shall do:

THE TRUTH ABOUT BOREDOM

"But it isn't easy," said Pooh. "Because
Poetry and Hums aren't things which
you get, they're things which get you.
And all you can do is to go where they
can find you."

—A. A. MILNE,
THE HOUSE AT POOH CORNER

Our brains do some very important work when we enter a place of
mind wandering or daydreaming.

When we constantly fill up all of our "empty" time with stimulation in the form of electronic devices, games, and distractions,
our brains become disengaged and the thinking process is effec-
tively halted. We never get to hear our own inner voice—we don't
develop a relationship with ourselves and our minds. We don't
get to know who we are because we're not listening.

But if we make a conscious effort to not distract ourselves, as
psychologist Sandi Mann says, "We might go off in our heads to
try and find that stimulation by our minds wandering, daydreaming." Through this process, we begin to think "a little bit beyond
the conscious, a little bit in the subconscious which allows sort of
different connections to take place."*

---

* "Bored . . . And Brilliant? A Challenge to Disconnect from Your Phone," NPR,
January 12, 2015. npr.org/sections/alltechconsidered/2015/01/12/376717870/
bored-and-brilliant-a-challenge-to-disconnect-from-your-phone.

Regular wandering provides us with mental space so that ideas have a chance to form.

When you start to feel that itch of needing to fill up that void and to check in online, remind yourself how good it feels to be in your body. Remind yourself that your mind is powerful only if you give it the space to ponder. Focus on the breath. The wanderer has power over his or her impulses.

> *In daydreams, which can occupy a third of our waking state, the brain becomes highly active in exactly those areas associated with complex problem-solving, because in daydreaming the mind roams freely, broadly and profoundly across one's life.*
>
> —JAY GRIFFITHS, A COUNTRY CALLED CHILDHOOD

For creativity, you need to let your mind wander.

Daydream as if your life depends on it.

Save your brain space for things that are important: your ideas, your daydreams, your experiments, your brainstorming, your exploration, your research.

I AM BEGINNING TO PAY ATTENTION TO MY URGE TO DISTRACT MYSELF AND TRY TO DETERMINE WHY IT OCCURS.

IT'S BEEN AN AMAZING WEEK OF WANDER SOCIETY FINDINGS! R AND I LOCATED ANOTHER STATION THAT CONTAINED A MINI ZINE. ALSO SPOTTED TWO SEPARATE ITEMS OF GRAFFITI. ONE WAS A QUOTE IN CHALK: "I WALKED MYSELF INTO MY BEST THOUGHTS." — SØREN KIERKEGAARD. THE OTHER, ANOTHER WHEAT PASTE POSTER OF WHITMAN. I HAVE BEEN SEEING IMAGES OF WALT WHITMAN EVERYWHERE— ON BUS SHELTERS, IN THE WOODS PASTED ON A ROCK, DOWNTOWN ON POSTS. EVERYTHING IN MY WORLD FEELS LIKE IT IS CONNECTED TO HIM AND THE WANDER SOCIETY. IS IT REAL OR IMAGINED? IS IT ME MAKING THESE CONNECTIONS OR IS THE UNIVERSE GUIDING ME?

REMEMBER

THE WANDER SOCIETY

FOR ALL KINDS OF CALM

ENTER

A

NEW PLANE

-OF-

EXISTENCE.

HOW TO SUMMON THE SPIRITS OF FELLOW WANDERERS

Qualities of great wanderers: curious, inquisitive, nonconformist, rebellious, daring, revolutionary, inventive, visionary, solitary, self-sufficient.

> *To be away from home and yet to find oneself everywhere at home; to see the world, to be at the centre of the world, and yet remain hidden from the world.*
>
> **—CHARLES BAUDELAIRE, THE PAINTER OF MODERN LIFE**

You will conjure the souls and energy of the great thinkers, creators, and writers during your wanderings. Their writings will offer a little light along your path (which can sometimes be murky).

To meet them, spend time in junky old bookshops. Find old dog-eared copies of their words to carry with you on your wanderings. The books will become friends who accompany you on the wandering path. The smell of the worn pages will offer comfort when you are in need of a lift.

Once you've decided who you'd like to meet, take a moment to quiet your mind. Breathe deeply. Think about who you might like to summon.

Say these words: "To the spirits of fellow wanderers, I am calling out to you for your wisdom and insight. Please help me find the ideas and solutions I am seeking. I will trust your guidance and remain open to whatever ideas you send to me, even if I don't understand them fully at the time."

Note: It is important to give thanks when the ideas do come in. You can leave an offering in a special spot, burn something, or just say "thank you."

THE WANDERER

He who has attained to only some degree of freedom of mind cannot feel other than a wanderer on the earth—though not as a traveller to a final destination; for this destination does not exist. But he will watch and observe and keep his eyes open to see what is really going on in the world; for this reason he may not let his heart adhere too firmly to any individual thing; within him too there must be something wandering that takes pleasure in change and transience.

—FRIEDRICH NIETZSCHE, HUMAN, ALL TOO HUMAN

AFTER READING THIS I LEFT AN OFFERING (SOME FLOWERS) AT A SECRET SPOT IN THE WOODS. I FEEL AS THOUGH WW IS HELPING ME, SENDING ME IDEAS, LEADING ME TO DISCOVERIES.

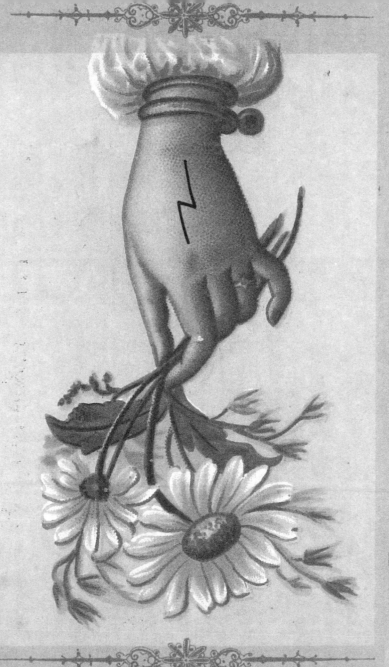

DO NOTHING, BUT LISTEN.

THE WANDERERS ARE EVERYWHERE.

FELLOW WANDERERS

Here are some of your partners on the wandering path:

WALT WHITMAN

(1819–1892) American writer Walt Whitman was one of the greatest wanderers and observers of all time, able to participate fully in his experience every time he went out into the world. It was rumored that he existed on a higher plane of consciousness than most people. People reported to be forever changed after spending time with him. His prose was the result of his daily roamings around the streets of New York City.

FERNANDO PESSOA

(1888–1935) Portuguese writer Fernando Pessoa once said, "I am a nomadic wanderer through my consciousness." Pessoa wandered through the streets of Lisbon, sometimes day and night. He was considered a flâneur, one who wanders aimlessly, and he wrote in the voice of seventy-five different heteronyms (imaginary characters).*

LUDWIG WITTGENSTEIN

(1889–1951) Austrian philosopher Ludwig Wittgenstein was known to stop mid-walk on the paths around Killary to draw various symbols in the mud with his walking stick.†

---

* "Walking on these streets, until the night falls, my life feels to me like the life they have. By day they're full of meaningless activity; by night they're full of meaningless lack of it. By day I am nothing, and by night I am I. There is no difference between me and these streets, save they being streets and I a soul, which perhaps is irrelevant when we consider the essence of things." Fernando Pessoa, *The Book of Disquiet*, edited and translated by Richard Zenith (New York: Penguin Books, 2003).

† Billy Mills, "Path to Enlightenment: How Walking Inspires Writers," *The Guardian*, August 9, 2012. theguardian.com/books/2012/aug/09/how-walking-inspires -writers.

NOTE TO RESEARCH PESSOA.

WILLIAM WORDSWORTH

(1770–1850) The great English Romantic poet William Wordsworth was known for his habit of walking, sometimes for up to five months at a time, with only one change of clothes and a pencil.

CHARLOTTE SMITH

(1749–1806) Charlotte Smith was an English Romantic poet and novelist. Her writing was inspired by her wanderings in the English countryside and along the shore. Smith's poems were also meandering, not linear, similar to the wandering state of mind that occurs when one is in a contemplative state.

CHARLES BAUDELAIRE

(1821–1867) French poet Charles Baudelaire has become a symbol of one who feels in his element while in a crowd. While not invented by Baudelaire, the concept of the flâneur—"wandering without aim, stopping once in a while to look around"—has been linked to both his character and his poetry. Baudelaire wandered the streets of Paris and in doing so became the voice of the flâneur.

HENRY DAVID THOREAU

(1817–1862) American writer and naturalist Henry David Thoreau is best known for his book *Walden*, which detailed his choice to live simply in nature for two years. As he puts it, "I wanted to live deep and suck out all the marrow of life."* Thoreau most exemplifies the wandering lifestyle through his philosophy of "living deliberately, being awake, and learning what the soul thrives on."

---

* "I went to the woods because I wished to live deliberately, to front only the essential facts of life, and see if I could not learn what it had to teach, and not, when I came to die, discover that I had not lived. I did not wish to live what was not life, living is so dear; nor did I wish to practise resignation, unless it was quite necessary. I wanted to live deep and suck out all the marrow of life, to live so sturdily and Spartan-like as to put to rout all that was not life, to cut a broad swath and shave close, to drive life into a corner, and reduce it to its lowest terms, and, if it proved to be mean, why then to get the whole and genuine meanness of it, and publish its meanness to the world; or if it were sublime, to know it by experience, and be able to give a true account of it in my next excursion." Henry David Thoreau, *Walden: or, Life in the Woods* (New York: Library of America, 2010).

WALTER BENJAMIN

(1892–1940) German philosopher Walter Benjamin promoted the idea of the flâneur in his commentaries on Baudelaire. Benjamin's idea of the flâneur is that of a wanderer in a modern city, one who needs the crowd yet is isolated by it. Benjamin himself was a wanderer of the streets of Paris and also a collector.

NASSIM TALEB

(1960–) Contemporary writer Nassim Taleb writes in the essay "Why I Walk" about how he partakes in lots of aimless wandering combined with short sprinting as a foundation for his "anti-fragile" lifestyle. He also writes at length about the need for randomness and variation, which he says creates resilience and strength.

ARISTOTLE

(384–322 BC) The great Greek thinker Aristotle founded the Peripatetic school of philosophy around 335 BC. *Peripatetic* means "one who walks habitually and extensively."[*] Members of his school followed a "tradition of meditative walking in which philosophical thought is in some way harnessed to the physical movements of the walker."[†]

PEACE PILGRIM

(1908–1981) American non-denominational spiritual leader and anti-war activist Peace Pilgrim wandered and walked across the United States and Canada for twenty-eight years, spreading the word of peace. She documented her philosophy and her travels in the book *Peace Pilgrim: Her Life and Work in Her Own Words.*[‡]

---

[*] Rebecca Solnit, *Wanderlust: A History of Walking* (New York: Viking, 2000).

[†] Ibid.

[‡] Peace Pilgrim, *Peace Pilgrim: Her Life and Work in Her Own Words* (Santa Fe, NM: Ocean Tree Books, 1992).

JOHN MUIR

(1838–1914)   Scottish-American naturalist and nature writer John Muir wrote about his explorations in nature (specifically the Sierra Nevada mountains of California), and devoted much of his life to the preservation of wilderness in the United States. Upon visiting Yosemite for the first time, Muir "was overwhelmed by the landscape, scrambling down steep cliff faces to get a closer look at the waterfalls, whooping and howling at the vistas, jumping tirelessly from flower to flower."*

---

* Amy Leinbach Marquis, "A Mountain Calling: John Muir's Ambles Through Wilderness Did More Than Just Appease His Wild Heart—They Revolutionized the Conservation Movement," *National Parks*, September 22, 2007.

JOSEPH MITCHELL

(1908–1996) American writer Joseph Mitchell spent his days wandering the streets of Manhattan. Through his walking he met many colorful characters and was known for his portraits of eccentrics and people on the fringes of society. He wrote, "What I really like to do is wander aimlessly in the city. I like to walk the streets by day and by night. It is more than a liking, a simple liking—it is an aberration."

VIRGINIA WOOLF

(1882–1941) Writer Virginia Woolf liked to spend her time during her youth "solitary trampling."[*] She said walking in the countryside allowed her to "have space to spread my mind out in." Later in life, wandering allowed her to escape the solitude of writing as well as her identity. She carried out much of her creative thinking and plotted her novels as she walked.

---

[*] "It has become the habit for me to spend my afternoons in solitary trampling. A great distance of the surrounding country have I now traversed thus, & the map of the land becomes solid in my brain." Virginia Woolf, *A Passionate Apprentice: The Early Journals, 1897–1909*, edited by Mitchell A. Leaska (San Diego: Harcourt Brace Jovanovich, 1990).

GUY DEBORD

(1931–1994) French Marxist theorist Guy Debord made urban exploration into a conscious experiment. He started the Situationist International in the 1950s, which participated in psychogeography, a method of moving around a city based on randomness, or "subordination of habitual influences." He also created the concept of *dérive* (French for "drifting") in which "one or more persons in a certain period drop their usual motives for movement and action, their relations, their work and leisure activities, and let themselves be drawn by the attractions of the terrain and the encounters they find there."[*]

---

[*] *Situationist International Anthology*, edited and translated by Ken Knabb (Berkeley, CA: Bureau of Public Secrets, 2006).

ARTHUR MACHEN

(1863–1947) Gothic horror writer Arthur Machen was known to write in the evening and go on long rambling walks across London. Machen once wrote, "Of all this the follower of the London Art must purge himself when he sets out on his adventures. For the essence of this art is that it must be an adventure into the unknown, and perhaps it may be found that this, at last, is the matter of all the arts."*

BASHŌ

(1644–1694) The great Japanese poet Bashō, who is credited with inventing the haiku, spent his life immersed in nature. After a year in which he went through many tragic circumstances and lost everything he had, Bashō took to the road. From the age of forty, he traveled from place to place teaching poetry in each town or village he entered.

THICH NHAT HANH

(1926–) Vietnamese Zen Buddhist monk Thich Nhat Hanh lives at the Plum Village Monastery in the south of France. He teaches and practices walking meditation all over the world. He once said, "To enjoy walking meditation isn't difficult at all. You don't need ten years of practicing mindful walking to be enlightened. You need

---

* Merlin Coverley, *The Art of Wandering: The Writer as Walker* (Harpenden, UK: Oldcastle Books, 2012).

only a few seconds. You just need to become aware that you are walking."*

SØREN KIERKEGAARD

(1813–1855) Danish philosopher Søren Kierkegaard used walking to inform his writing. He would write until noon every day and then wander the streets of Copenhagen, observing with a keen eye. "When you go for a walk, let your thoughts wander aimlessly, snooping about, experimenting with first one thing and then another," he instructed.[†]

ALICE P. HOBBS

(1980–) Contemporary artist and avid collector Alice P. Hobbs's story is shrouded in mystery and has been cause for much speculation. Hobbs's work is informed by her daily wanderings around an undisclosed city as documented in a hard-to-find book entitled *In the Realms of the Unexplored*. While not much background information exists on the artist, she has developed a wide group of devoted followers who seek to uncover more about her life, process, and whereabouts.[‡]

---

* Thich Nhat Hanh, *How to Walk* (Berkeley, CA: Parallax Press, 2015).
† Niels Jørgen Cappelørn, et al., *Written Images: Søren Kierkegaard's Journals, Notebooks, Booklets, Sheets, Scraps, and Slips of Paper* (Princeton, NJ: Princeton University Press, 2003).
‡ Read more at whoisalicephobbs.com.

SOME MORE WANDERERS FOR YOU TO EXPLORE

GEORGE ORWELL (1903–1950): an English writer whose work focused on social justice.

THOMAS DE QUINCEY (1785–1859): an English essayist best known for his reflections on addiction and the self.

BRUCE CHATWIN (1940–1989): an English writer whose wanderings took him all over the world and earned him the label "travel writer," a label he rejected.

W. G. SEBALD (1944–2001): a German academic and writer whose works explored themes of memory and decay of civilizations, traditions, and objects.

CHARLES DICKENS (1812–1870): an English writer and literary personality who criticized the harsh social stratification of society.

GRAHAM GREENE (1904–1991): an English author and spy who traveled the world to visit and write about remote places and adventures while collecting intelligence.

OSCAR WILDE (1854–1900): an Irish playwright, poet, and personality who became well-known for his wit and style and who advocated for experiencing all that life had to offer.

ARTHUR RIMBAUD (1854–1891): a French poet known for his reputation as a libertine who traveled widely on three continents.

GERTRUDE STEIN (1874–1946): an American writer who traveled across the United States before eventually settling in Europe.

GEORGES PEREC (1936–1982): a French writer and filmmaker whose work was highly experimental.

FRIEDRICH NIETZSCHE (1844–1900): a German philosopher who expounded ideas that questioned truth and promoted transcendence beyond structure.

JEAN-JACQUES ROUSSEAU (1712–1778): a Genevan-French philosopher who inspired the ideals of the French Revolution.

LANGSTON HUGHES (1902–1967): an American writer and social activist who traveled widely throughout the world and was a leader of the Harlem Renaissance.

C. S. LEWIS (1898–1963): an Irish-English novelist and theologian best known for his novels about the fantastical world of Narnia.

HERMANN HESSE (1877–1962): a Swiss poet and novelist whose work explored themes of the individual's search for self-knowledge and spirituality.

REBECCA SOLNIT (1961–): an American writer who was educated in the United States and Europe and has become a prominent activist for environmental and social change.

ROBERT WALSER (1878–1956): a Swiss modernist writer whose works blend playful serenity with existential exploration.

GARY SNYDER (1930–): an American academic and writer who travels the world and writes about his immersions in different spiritual cultures and in nature.

JACK KEROUAC (1922–1969): an American poet and novelist of the Beat Generation, best known for his book *On the Road*, based on his travels across America with his friends.

ROBERT LOUIS STEVENSON (1850–1894): a Scottish novelist and travel writer whose work took him across Europe and North America.

LUDWIG VAN BEETHOVEN (1770–1827): a German pianist and one of the most famous and influential composers of all time.

JAMES JOYCE (1882–1941): an Irish novelist and poet best known for *Ulysses*, a modernist work in which he explored the episodes of Homer's *Odyssey* in a variety of literary styles.

MICHEL DE CERTEAU (1925–1986): a French Jesuit and scholar best known for *The Practice of Everyday Life*, which mused on a study of the repetitive and unconscious aspects of life.

RICHARD JEFFERIES (1848–1887): an English nature writer best known for his personal writings about rural life in the English countryside. His notable book *The Story of My Heart* was recently republished with notes by authors Brooke Williams and Terry Tempest Williams.

WERNER HERZOG (1942–): a German filmmaker known for filming in far-flung locations and using locals in his film projects to benefit what he calls "ecstatic truth."

WILLIAM BLAKE (1757–1827): an English poet, painter, and printmaker whose diverse body of work embraced imagination.

NICK PAPADIMITRIOU (1959–): an Englishman known as the "London Perambulator" who explores and archives the unknown through walking.

WILL SELF (1961–): a British novelist and journalist. Self-described as a psychogeographer and a flâneur and has written about his many walking adventures.

ROBERT MACFARLANE (1976–): a British travel writer who wrote *The Old Ways: A Journey on Foot*.

GEOFF NICHOLSON (1953–): a British novelist and nonfiction writer; author of *The Lost Art of Walking*.

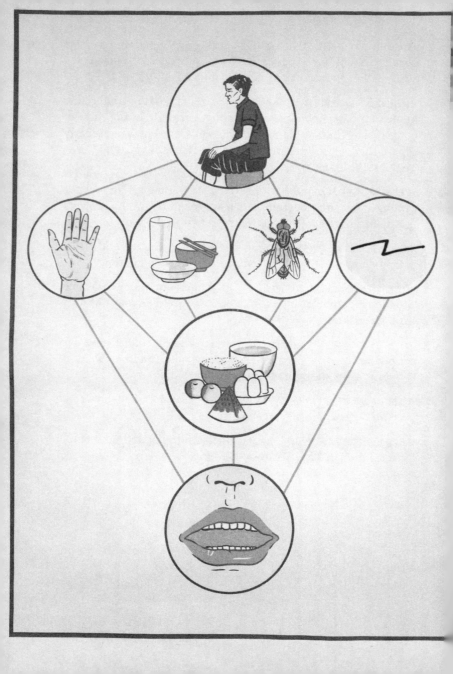

THE WANDER SOCIETY'S TACTICAL GUIDE

YOU HAVE ARRIVED

There should be no cackle of voices at
your elbow, to jar on the meditative
silence of the morning. You must be
open to all impressions and let your
thoughts take color from what you see.

—ROBERT LOUIS STEVENSON

I'VE BEEN RESEARCHING HOW WE RECEIVE SENSORY INFORMATION
THROUGH OUR BODIES (NOT JUST OUR EYES & HANDS). "YOU HAVE TO
TRUST THE THINGS YOU CAN'T NAME. YOU FEEL THROUGH YOUR BODY,
YOU TAKE IN THE WORLD THROUGH YOUR SKIN." — ANN HAMILTON,
ARTIST.   WHAT IF THE WORLD IS COMMUNICATING TO US IN WAYS
WE ARE NOT EVEN AWARE OF?

ENTER THE UNKNOWN

THE WANDERING ESSENTIALS

The wanderer follows the guidance of Henry David Thoreau, who moved to the woods for a year to determine what made for a fulfilling life. His intent was to "live deep and suck the marrow out of life" and to, as he put it, "live deliberately, to front only the essential facts of life, and see if I could not learn what it had to teach, and not, when I came to die, discover that I had not lived." This is also the quest of the wanderer, to live deliberately, to be awake, to figure out what our soul thrives on.

One of the most important conclusions Thoreau came to is that we actually need very few things. He approached material goods from the perspective of how little can we get by with rather than how much can we acquire. This paring down and questioning is also the path of the wanderer.

If it is true that we value soul life above everything else, then at some point we must consider the value of our time over the need to make money. Money does not help us to develop our soul. Of technology Thoreau wrote, "Our inventions are wont to be pretty toys, which distract our attention from serious things."

How little do we need to lead a life that feeds our soul? What if we altered our value system so that priority was placed on soul-enhancing endeavors such as skill building, self-sufficiency, exploration, research, mind-expanding tasks? Imagine how

MORE SIGHTINGS TODAY. MY FRIEND R FOUND SOME MORE MINI ZINES. ONE WAS IN THE BOOKSTORE ON A SHELF. ANOTHER ON THE SIDEWALK OUTSIDE. STARTING TO FEEL LIKE THE WANDER SOCIETY IS SEEKING US OUT INSTEAD OF THE OTHER WAY AROUND.

different our society would be if we placed priority on these things instead of wealth creation, technology, and material acquisition.

The relinquishment of the need to make more money than we need allows us the greatest freedom.

What if you needed something and could build it for yourself out of things that you already had around you or things you could easily acquire? This is possible.

Once our bases are covered—food, shelter, clothing—we have everything we need. How little can you live with?

Instead of following the path outlined by society, we can find alternatives.

If you are interested in clothing and fashion, could you learn to make your own or alter existing clothing as opposed to buying new things?

If you need a chair, could you teach yourself to make one? What are the most basic requirements of a chair? Does it have to be in the form that society tells us? Some of the most interesting spaces are created out of a need to use readily available materials.

As wanderers, our goal is to pare down our essentials to as few things as possible. The questions we should ask ourselves with each thing are "Does this add to my idea of a soulful existence?," "Do I love this object?," "Will this object add to my life or will it weigh it down?," "Does this object help me in my pursuit of a wanderer's lifestyle?"

"How can I embody Thoreau's mandate to 'live deliberately'?"

HAD A LONG CONVERSATION WITH J. TINDLEBAUM ABOUT THE BOOK. TOLD HIM ABOUT OUR RECENT DISCOVERIES. HE SEEMED EXCITED. WE WILL BE MEETING IN PERSON SO HE CAN EXAMINE THEM.

Passing, glimpsing, everything seems accidentally but miraculously sprinkled with beauty.

—Virginia Woolf

UNPLANNED TIME

The world believes that time is standard. But this is a myth.

Have you noticed that it changes dramatically depending on the tasks you are conducting? There is time based on society and time experienced by the psyche. These are very different.

> *Imagine time as a landscape: long hills of open after-noons, unfenced horizons of hours, the vast and immacu-late freedom of time which, until so very recently, all of humanity knew. But foreshorten the horizons, fence the days, restrict the hours, erect deadline, add punctuality, alarm clocks and speed—enclose the commons of time, in other word—and people will feel pressured, even if they know how to live in a clock-driven world.*
>
> **—JAY GRIFFITHS, A COUNTRY CALLED CHILDHOOD**

Think back to childhood, when time seemed to stretch out infinitely and lazily, allowing space for the unplanned and unpredictable. This is time as experienced by the psyche.

Now, think about your schedule today, how it is dictated by time-based requirements: work, school, etc. This is time based on society.

The wanderer does not operate outside of society, but has no need to partake in its time-based requirements while wandering.

ANOTHER WAY TO
CONSIDER TIME AS A WANDERER

The ancient Greeks thought of time in two different ways: *chronos* and *kairos*. *Chronos* referred to sequential time, while *kairos* referred to nonlinear time—the opportune moment. *As wanderers we worship the god Kairos, "the god of timing, of chance and mischance, the god of the special moment, the colorful, the variegated time of the psyche,"* says Jay Griffiths in *A Country Called Childhood*.

The wanderer does not attempt to control time, but rather lets it unfurl as it may, existing in kairos, not chronos.

> *Walking takes longer than any other form of locomotion except crawling. Thus, it stretches time and prolongs life. Walking makes the world much bigger, and therefore more interesting. You have time to observe the details.*
>
> —*EDWARD ABBEY*, THE JOURNEY HOME

I'M ON "WANDER TIME." TIME IS CHANGING FOR ME. I HAVE A BIT MORE BREATHING SPACE.

THE WANDERERS
ARE EVERYWHERE

SECRECY,
OR HOW TO BE INVISIBLE

The Wander Society conducts all of its operations in a covert fashion. This is for a variety of reasons:

Society does not understand the concept of unplanned time or non-planning. You may be criticized, judged, or ridiculed for your activities. This is best avoided altogether.

No one needs to know about your wanderings. It is okay to have something that is just yours.

Your thoughts are powerful and need time to emerge without distractions. This can only be done in a solitary fashion.

Wandering is an ancient and powerful tool. When you wander you are connecting with a group of great thinkers who used this tool to further humankind and for good. **This path is not for everyone.** You are entrusted with the knowledge of its power and should only pass on this knowledge to others who are able to honor it.

Secrecy allows members to conduct research quietly and covertly.

> *She had the oddest sense of being herself invisible; unseen; unknown.*
>
> —*VIRGINIA WOOLF, MRS. DALLOWAY*

MET WITH R THIS AFTERNOON. SHE FEELS HERSELF GOING FURTHER INTO THE WS EXPERIENCE. THOUGH HARD TO PUT INTO WORDS WHAT THIS MEANS.

You may want to incorporate secrecy in your wanderings if you are on a secret mission and plan to leave something in the environment that wasn't there before. Or perhaps you want to wander silently at full attention, preferring not to be interrupted. You may also want to go unnoticed by others because it is like a superpower of sorts (that is, you are experimenting with being a spy).

Choosing to be invisible is not an attempt to ignore your individuality, nor is it about denying your own personal qualities. It is actually a choice to take a position of strength and creative control over your surroundings, while also demonstrating a level of respect for the natural world.

Being invisible is also a way to fit into your surroundings much like animals do. This power makes you more adaptable to the environment and the present moment/situation.

METHODS
1. Camouflage. Hide in plain sight. Dress plainly, in bland colors so as not to attract attention. You are an animal in the wild, able to blend into your surroundings when needed.
2. Adapting to the rhythm of a place. Go at the pace of nature. Move slowly or swiftly when needed.
3. Practice silent movement.
4. Do not wear perfumes or strong smelling products of any kind.
5. Keep your stuff to a minimum. Carrying only a few items makes you more mobile and agile.
6. Participate in activities that others are doing so as to blend into the environment.

ANOTHER EXAMPLE OF EVERYTHING FEELING CONNECTED. I FIND MYSELF READING BOOKS AND WONDERING IF THE WRITER MAY BE A MEMBER OF TWS. IT FEELS AS IF THERE ARE CLUES HIDDEN IN THE TEXT. REFERENCES TO WHITMAN OR WORDSWORTH.

OBSERVATION, OR NATURE AS TEACHER

When you go out to enjoy nature, leave
all expectations behind. Be
spontaneous. Look at everything with
equal curiosity. Go to the woods for the
sheer enjoyment of experiencing
anything. Then everything will be a
source of wonder and enjoyment.

—TOM BROWN, *TOM BROWN'S FIELD
GUIDE TO LIVING WITH THE EARTH*

We depend on technology and science to get us around, to allow us to control and keep at bay the wild world. But while technology can help us in some ways, it also serves to keep the natural world at a distance. It causes our senses and our natural navigating techniques to become lost or at the very least dulled. To exist directly in the natural world now makes us feel vulnerable, fearful.

It is only when we are fully present that we can begin to connect with the natural world again, and in the process, get in touch with our animal selves, with the alive and alert part of ourselves that senses and notices everything in front of us: trees, sidewalk, bird sounds, wind, cats, movement, concrete, feet hitting the ground.

We can train ourselves to get in the habit of being present. We can train ourselves to notice the small details. It just requires practice.

Begin by observing. Sit quietly in any location. Tune into the nature around you. How are things interacting? What happens when there is a disturbance? Consider that this interaction is happening constantly, every day, all day. All living things are connected and interacting at all times.

The nature writer Tom Brown always asks the question: What is the landscape telling me? We can look at it like a giant puzzle, by observing movement, smells, interactions, plant life, tree habitat, age of trees. We can look at it from many different angles.

Every landscape is a rich source of information.

Look for clues that might tell you about who or what and how someone is using the space. Tracks, marks, leave behinds, detritus, paths. How have humans altered a space? What can you smell? What can the smells tell you? What is the quality of the light? Study the plant life. What grows here? What can the trees tell you? Is the color of the bark uniform or does it change depending on some outside force? Do you notice any patterns? How does the weather change the scene?

In the beginning you might feel like there is not much to see, but if you give it time the natural world will reveal its magic to you. Begin to record your findings; this will allow you to track changes.

By sitting in one spot, we can begin to feel the rhythm of a place. Give yourself time. Visit the same spot regularly. You will begin to see that the world is infinitely fascinating and full of things that you didn't notice on first sight.

MADE AN AMAZING DISCOVERY TODAY AFTER FOLLOWING A SMALL DIRT ROAD NEAR MY HOUSE. AFTER PASSING INTO A GULLY, I FOUND A MAGICAL LITTLE CREEK RUNNING THROUGH IT. THREE YEARS HERE AND I'D NEVER SEEN IT BEFORE!

Note: The Wander Society strongly recommends the book *The Walker's Guide to Outdoor Clues & Signs* by Tristan Gooley. This will help you gain skills as a natural navigator and observer.

It will also give you many insights into the small details and what to look for as a wanderer. Before long you will be an expert.

> One small clue can change the way you think about your surroundings quite dramatically.
>
> —TRISTAN GOOLEY,
> THE WALKER'S GUIDE TO OUTDOOR CLUES & SIGNS

BOOK HAS BEEN ACQUIRED! BEEN PAYING ATTENTION TO MOSS AND LICHEN ON TREES.

THE PATH IS HOME

WANDERING MEDITATION

Wandering meditation is a form of meditation that involves physical activity and focusing on the movement itself. This form of meditation is also referred to as nondirective meditation.

When you wander, try to keep your awareness on the experience of walking. Pay attention to the feeling of the soles of your feet hitting the ground. If your mind wanders, it is okay, just bring your focus back to the body and the movement.

Wanderers are encouraged to do this kind of meditation because it helps develop a greater awareness and allows us to experience deep fulfillment. Over time we can bring this experience into our everyday lives.

When you walk, arrive with every step. That is walking meditation. There is nothing else to it.

—THICH NHAT HANH, HOW TO WALK

R AND I HAVE CREATED OUR OWN WANDER SOCIETY
MESSAGE STATION (OLD LOG WITH HOLES IN IT). WE HAVE
BEEN USING IT TO COMMUNICATE WITH EACH OTHER. TINY
NOTES HIDDEN IN THE HOLES.

THE WANDERER
AND TECHNOLOGY

Technology can be used as a way to
avoid direct encounter, as a shield—
etched with lines of code or cryptic
jargon—to ward off whatever frightens,
as a synthetic heaven or haven in which
to hide out from the distressing
ambiguity of the real.

—DAVID ABRAM, *BECOMING ANIMAL*

Technology can be an amazing tool when used for good. But when it is used constantly throughout your day, it serves to distract and disconnect you from the things you are attempting to explore on a deep level, namely yourself and the world.

On this note, the wanderer makes a conscious decision to limit his or her technology use while out on wanderings. Certainly technology will be used for documentation purposes, but other access should be limited to emergency use only. The exception is if you are conducting research on a particular subject or practicing skill building and need to access a tutorial, pattern, instructions, etc.

BEWARE THE TECHNOLOGY TRAP

In his 2004 book *A Short History of Progress*, author Ronald Wright wrote about a concept called the "progress trap." A progress trap is the pursuit of progress through human ingenuity (often through using technology) that results in humans creating more problems for themselves in the long run.

A technology trap is similar. In the pursuit of increased productivity and success humans implement the use of more technology, which results in creating more time spent using technology, which often results in decreased productivity. If the same amount of time was spent doing the thing that needs to be done, instead of doing things surrounding the thing that needs to be done (organizing, planning, learning a new technology, thinking about working), then productivity might actually be increased.

THE TECHNOLOGY TRAP IS ONE OF MY GREATEST CHALLENGES. I HAVE PROVEN TO MYSELF THAT I AM MUCH BETTER WITHOUT IT. THE BEST SOLUTION FOR ME IS TO LIMIT IT AS MUCH AS POSSIBLE (CHECK EMAIL ONCE OR TWICE A DAY). MUST CONTINUE WITH THIS.

READ, OR WANDERING LIBRARY, OR THE GATEWAY TO OTHER WORLDS

PLACES FOR YOU TO EXPLORE ON YOUR WANDERINGS

Reading books is an essential tool for skill building as a wanderer. It allows us to explore virtually any skill we wish to learn. And we can do it in the midst of our wanderings. Consider yourself a scholar in the University of Everyday Life. The Wander Society recommends the following books:

Edward Abbey, *The Journey Home*
David Abram, *Becoming Animal*
Gaston Bachelard, *The Poetics of Space*
Charles Baudelaire, *The Painter of Modern Life and Other Essays*
Tom Brown, *Tom Brown's Field Guide to Living with the Earth*
Richard Maurice Bucke, *Cosmic Consciousness*
Italo Calvino, *If on a Winter's Night a Traveler*
Joseph Campbell, *The Hero with a Thousand Faces*
Niels Jørgen Cappelørn, et al., *Written Images: Søren Kierkegaard's Journals, Notebooks, Booklets, Sheets, Scraps, and Slips of Paper*
Merlin Coverley, *The Art of Wandering: The Writer as Walker*
Matthew Crawford, *Shop Class as Soulcraft*
Guy Debord, *Society of the Spectacle*
Emily Dickinson, *The Complete Poems of Emily Dickinson*
Annie Dillard, *Pilgrim at Tinker Creek*

Ralph Waldo Emerson, *The Essential Writings of Ralph Waldo Emerson*

Tristan Gooley, *The Natural Navigator*

Tristan Gooley, *The Walker's Guide to Outdoor Clues & Signs*

Jay Griffiths, *A Country Called Childhood*

Frédéric Gros, *A Philosophy of Walking*

Thich Nhat Hanh, *How to Walk*

Thich Nhat Hanh, *Peace Is Every Step*

Hermann Hesse, *Wandering: Notes and Sketches*

C. G. Jung, *The Earth Has a Soul: The Nature Writings of C. G. Jung*

Ken Knabb, *Situationist International Anthology*

James Lord, *Giacometti: A Biography*

A. A. Milne, *The House at Pooh Corner*

John Muir, *John of the Mountains: The Unpublished Journals of John Muir*

Friedrich Nietzsche, *Human, All Too Human: A Book for Free Spirits*

Georges Perec, *Life: A User's Manual*

Georges Perec, *The Species of Spaces and Other Pieces*

Fernando Pessoa, *The Book of Disquiet*

Tom Robbins, *Skinny Legs and All*

R. Murray Schafer, *The Soundscape*

Will Self, *Psychogeography*

Maurice Sendak, *Where the Wild Things Are*

Gary Snyder, *Writers and the War Against Nature*

Rebecca Solnit, *A Field Guide to Getting Lost*

David G. Stern, *Wittgenstein's Philosophical Investigations*

Nassim Taleb, "How Things Gain from Disorder" (lecture: Stanford Technology Ventures Program, April 10, 2013)

Henry David Thoreau, *Walden: or, Life in the Woods*

Robert Walser, *The Walk*

Walt Whitman, *Song of Myself*

Virginia Woolf, *A Passionate Apprentice: The Early Journals, 1897–1909*

As many other works of fiction as you can fit in.

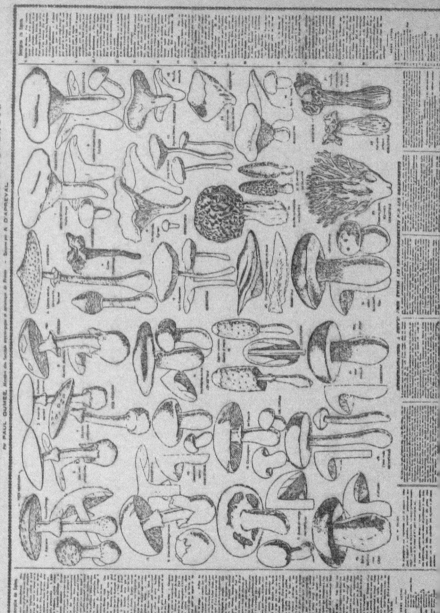

SKILL BUILDING, OR BECOMING AN AUTODIDACT

Note: *The skill-building component is not a mandatory requirement for Wander Society members. Partake in it only if you are drawn to doing so. However, the fact you are here implies that you probably will be.*

A consumerist system creates a belief in the "scarcity within," the belief that we need material goods to invoke the imagination, that we are incapable of constructing our own lives out of whatever we have at our disposal, that only others can provide us with the things needed to live. We learn that lifestyle is something to be bought, not created. Over time this belief can cause depression and a lack of meaning.

Members of the Wander Society adopt a self-sufficient mentality and a belief in the "resiliency within." Wanderers believe in the ability to exist and flourish wherever they are, using what they have. They use only what they need, nothing more (they do not understand the concept of excess, because that is a societal

HAVE DISCOVERED A NEW LEAD (CLUE) TO THE IDENTITY OF THE WANDER SOCIETY. ONE OF THE MINI ZINES HAD A PHONE NUMBER! WE CALLED AND LISTENED TO THE MESSAGE. 978-203-5503

construct). They do not fear the unknown, because they have learned that they are fully able to deal with the unexpected and respond to whatever situation arises.

As members of the Wander Society, it is important to teach ourselves skills that we can use to foster nomadic self-sufficiency, to believe we have immense powers and the ability to create whatever we might need in our travels.

Know this: *You are amazingly resourceful and adaptable.*

Whatever it is that you desire to learn is ready to be explored and researched. A trip to the library or bookstore or a Google search can set you on the path.

Some examples of self-sufficiency skills/crafts:

- Knitting
- Woodworking/whittling
- Coding/hacking
- Metal working
- Sewing
- Reading/research
- Writing
- Drawing
- Photography
- Music
- Printmaking (stamp carving)
- Weaving

R NOTICED SOME NUMBERS ON ONE OF THE ZINES!
(40.702545, -73.993746) WE PLUGGED THEM INTO
GOOGLE AND FOUND IT TO BE 28 OLD FULTON STREET,
BROOKLYN, NY. WITH MORE RESEARCH, WE DETERMINED
THIS IS THE SITE OF A BUILDING WW WORKED AT AS
AN EDITOR! R IS PLANNING A TRIP TO INVESTIGATE. WHAT IF
THERE IS SOMETHING THERE? COULD IT LEAD TO A NEW FIND?
WHY ELSE WOULD IT BE LISTED?

Choose something that really speaks to you. While it may seem daunting at first to learn a new skill, the sense of satisfaction that comes from teaching yourself something will be your reward.

VOL. I

REPOSITORY
of
Literature

THE WANDER
SOCIETY

SOLVITUR AMBULANDO

TO ALL MEMBERS, TAKE WHAT YOU CAN. PASS IT
ON TO OTHERS. THE UNIVERSE DEPENDS ON YOU.

WANDERING INITIATION

Chance furnished me what I need, I am like a man who stumbles along; my foot strikes something. I bend over, and it is exactly what I need.

—JAMES JOYCE, *ULYSSES*

THE WANDER SOCIETY

WE ARE EVERYWHERE

SETTING OUT

When you first start to wander, it is quite normal to feel a bit scattered or disconnected. You may think it is not a good time to wander, or that it would be better to be doing something else, anything else. This is the task-oriented part of your brain telling you this. Your inner critic may also be chiming in, telling you you're not doing it right, that you should abandon the whole idea.

Know this: *It takes time to ease into a wander.* This cannot be stressed enough! The beginning might feel forced or uncomfortable, the body tight, the mind wild. You must walk for a specific period of time before you feel the wander start to flow. The amount of time will vary depending on how engaged your mind is with your "real world" obligations. You must give yourself time to get into a rhythm.

But slowly, slowly, you can begin to notice things around you. Use your senses. How many different smells do you notice? What are the sounds you can hear right now? Listen to the sound your feet make when they touch the ground. Can you see any wildlife? Nature? Notice the pressure you feel when you place your foot down on the ground. Notice your breath. You may breathe a bit deeper now than you did a couple of minutes ago. You start to sink into a pace that feels good. Not too fast, not too slow. Enjoy the rhythm.

THE PORTABLE
RESEARCH STATION

> I never knew I was creating a world
> which was an antithesis to the world
> around me which was full of sorrows,
> full of wars, full of difficulties. I was
> creating the world I wanted, and into
> this world, once it is created, you
> invited others and then you attract
> those who have affinities and this
> becomes a universe.
>
> —ANAÏS NIN, *THE DIARY OF ANAÏS NIN*

Wanderers have a nomadic existence when out in the world. They are encouraged to bring with them items that foster this state of being so they can make themselves feel at home wherever they are. The wanderer also must be able to conduct research at any given moment. To this effect we must carry items that allow us to do this as efficiently and naturally as possible.

- **Bag.** Think of the bag as the foundation for your portable world. It should be big enough to carry the necessary items, but not too big that it is cumbersome when full. It should be able to hold your extra clothing layers when removed.

- **Uniform.** The uniform should consist of clothing that makes you feel most like yourself. It should be practical and adaptable to changes in the weather. Layers are recommended for this. See "On Creating a Uniform" on page 85.

- **Tools.** Carry with you a notebook/journal, writing utensils, sound-recording technology, camera, collecting containers (jars, boxes, or bags), binoculars, and a magnifying glass.

- **Talisman.** See "How to Find a Talisman" on page 87.

- **Food.** Choose food that gives you lots of energy. Natural options—food that isn't processed or altered—are best for this.

- **Books.** Carry one or two books that you are obsessed with. These can be books by fellow wanderers or perhaps books by kindred spirits.

- **A simple plant press.** You can also use a book for this purpose.

If you wish to experiment with a more involved nomadic experience, here are a few ideas:

- Portable tea brewing
- Portable napping
- Wild food foraging
- Remote broadcasting
- DIY cartography

R TOOK A PILGRIMAGE TO BROOKLYN TODAY. EXCITED TO SEE WHAT DEVELOPS. THERE APPEARS TO BE A BIG PRESENCE OF TWS IN NYC JUDGING BY THE SIGHTINGS ON PROFESSOR TINDLEBAUM'S WEBSITE, WWW.JTINDLEBAUM.NET.

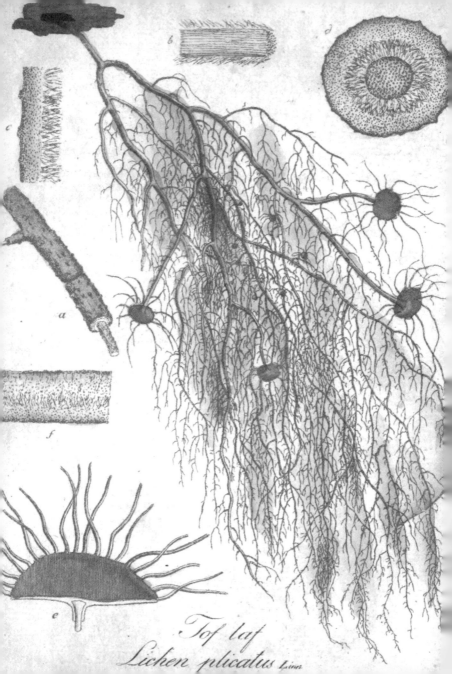

Tof laf

Lichen plicatus Linn

ON CREATING A UNIFORM

The purpose of ritual is to let your soul know that it is about to do something different than before, something important. Like gathering special tools and objects that we need for our quest, we can also do this by wearing something slightly different than what we normally do. The uniform does not have to look like a uniform; it only has to feel slightly different to you. There are easy ways to make your daily dress feel a little special or important. You do not need to make it obvious—it is more important for you to feel the change than to have others see it.

Here are some ideas for creating your uniform:

- Consider adding a scarf, bag/backpack, hat, jacket, T-shirt, and/or walking stick.
- Create and add a badge (see page 135) to hide somewhere on your person.
- Add secret pockets; these can be helpful to house your collections. Or they can be used to hold pieces of writing.
- Add some visible mending, or add your own details to a piece of clothing: a small square of fabric sewn onto a T-shirt or a hidden secret note sewn to the inside of a coat.

BEEN WAITING TO HEAR FROM R. NO WORD YET. SO CURIOUS.

HOW TO FIND A TALISMAN

A talisman is an object that is believed to have magical properties or some special significance for the carrier. It may bring luck, provide good energy, or offer some calm during challenging moments. A talisman should only be found or created by the person who intends to use it.

Ideas for talisman forms:

- Painted rock
- Wrapped bird feather(s)
- Carved stick
- Origami
- Found coin
- Jewelry (made by you)
- Paper talismans, for example an *ofuda*—a Japanese talisman made by inscribing a piece of paper or cloth with a name or symbol, used for good luck or to protect the user

Note: In choosing a talisman, you might select something that is visually appealing, something that feels good in your hand, or something that resonates with you emotionally. It is sometimes difficult to seek out a talisman. If you are finding this to be the case, it may be better if you allow it to come to you when the time is right. You should not force these things.

STILL NO WORD FROM R.
UPDATE: JUST RECEIVED AN EMAIL FROM R. VERY BRIEF.
"HI. SORRY FOR LACK OF COMMUNICATION. IT'S BEEN A
BIT HECTIC. MADE AN EXCITING DISCOVERY. TWS WAS
HERE. MORE TO TELL, BUT IT WILL HAVE TO WAIT UNTIL
I RETURN. SOLVITUR AMBULANDO."

HOW TO HAVE A DEEP REST IN THE MIDST OF WANDERING

After spending your time wandering for a while you will need to recharge, especially if you have traveled far from home and have a long way back. This happens often with wandering: We can be so enjoying the present moment that we end up going much farther than we intended and find ourselves needing rest, even for a few minutes. You will be amazed at how a little rest can give you the energy to carry on.

For many it can be challenging to take a nap in public. The feeling of self-consciousness prevents us from letting go completely. We are going to combat that as best as we can with these tools.

1. Find a comfortable location, somewhere you can lean back and rest your head. Sitting under a tree works well for this.

2. Secure belongings so that you will not worry about someone taking them in case you do go into a deep sleep.

3. Close your eyes and notice how good it feels to rest after all the movement you have been doing. Feel your body begin to let go of any tension. Feel the ground beneath you. Focus on your breathing.

4. It is not necessary that you drift off completely. What we are aiming for is that you enter one of the early stages of sleep. The first stage is the transition between wakefulness and sleep (people who are awoken during this stage will say that they were not asleep). The second stage is light sleep or the onset of sleep. You become disengaged from your surroundings, and your breathing and heart rate become regular. There are processes occurring during this phase that are replenishing to the body and brain.

5. Attempt this for at least ten minutes.

6. Come back to the world feeling refreshed!

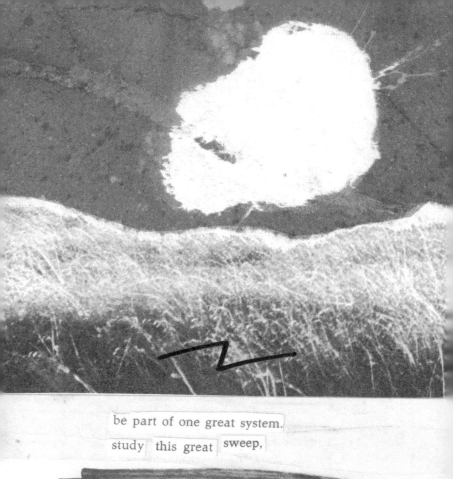

be part of one great system.

study this great sweep,

haphazard remnants yield a clue;

HOW TO INVOKE THE INNER WANDERER IN ANY SITUATION

We can invoke the inner wanderer whenever necessary, during challenging times, when we are feeling uncentered or fearful.

1. Begin by taking a deep breath.
2. Feel the ground beneath your feet (or beneath your body if you are lying down).
3. Tune into each of these senses: smells, sounds, touch, sights.
4. Feel the energy flowing through your body. Remember that your body holds an incredible amount of power and that you are infinitely strong and adaptable, even if you might not feel like it in the moment.
5. Continue to focus on your breathing for as long as possible. Let your mind wander while breathing.
6. Summon the spirit of your favorite writer or thinker. Ask them for help. Take on some of their power.
7. Picture your favorite place to wander. Go there in your mind. Conjure everything about it: smells, sounds, touch, sights.

HAVE BEEN THINKING LATELY ABOUT HOW, UNLESS YOU ARE IN AN URBAN SETTING, WANDERING IS VIEWED AS SOCIALLY UNACCEPTABLE OR IS FROWNED UPON. IT SHOULD BE THE OPPOSITE. PARTICULARLY WHEN WE ARE TRYING TO LIVE MORE SUSTAINABLY.

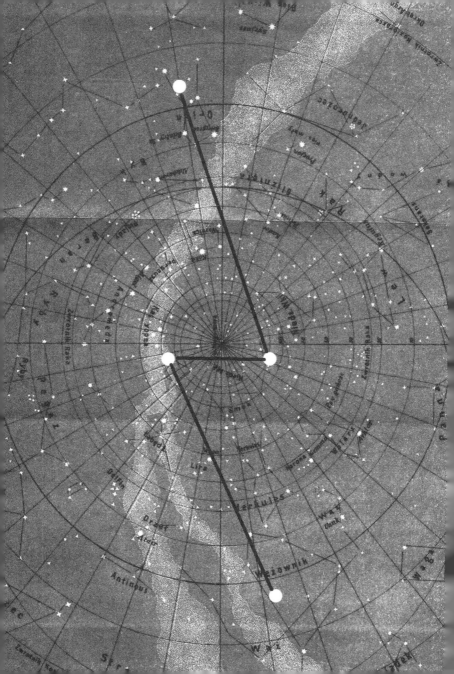

ASSIGNMENTS/ RESEARCH/ FIELD WORK

Let the wild rumpus start!

—MAURICE SENDAK,
WHERE THE WILD THINGS ARE

A regular wandering practice can be as simple as going out every day and letting the mind wander. But there are times when you might wish to use wandering as a way to foster creative play. Consider these assignments as experiments to try. Document all findings in your journal. Feel free to alter them to suit your needs.

R RETURNS HOME TODAY. EXCITED TO HEAR ABOUT HER ADVENTURE. MADE A WANDER SOCIETY PATCH TODAY. SEWED IT ONTO MY BAG.

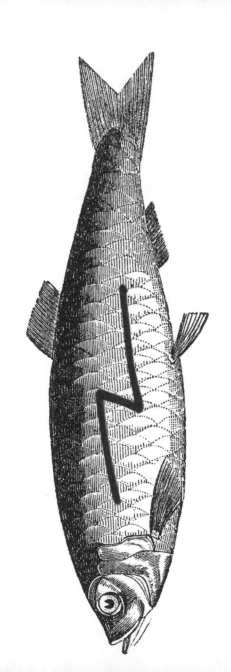

DOCUMENT EVERYTHING

You may decide to sit somewhere during your wandering to write down all you can remember. Or you can document as you go. Documenting choices: writing, photos, drawing, video, sound recordings.

Record it all.

SLOW WANDERING

Slow down your pace to at least half speed, slower if you can. Feel your feet touching the ground. Look at the ground. How much more do you see at this pace? This is a very different way of moving about the world. There is no need to speed up. Everything you need is right here.

WANDERER'S FILMOGRAPHY

Create a video based on . . .

. . . movement

. . . your feet

. . . cracks

. . . street signs

. . . found shapes

. . . secret locations

COLOR TRACKING

Spend one wandering session tracking one specific color. Take photos. Give a name to each of these sessions (the white session, the blue session). Print out the photos and put them in your journal.

MET R FOR COFFEE. SHE PRESENTED ME WITH A LARGE NEWSLETTER FROM TWS! MORE MATERIAL TO MINE FOR INFO. HER EXPERIENCE IN BROOKLYN HAS OPENED UP SOME MORE QUESTIONS. IT IS TOO LONG TO WRITE ABOUT HERE. SEE PAGE 175.

SOUND TRACKING

Spend a wandering session recording found sounds. Create your own "sound library." This research may be used later if you need to re-create a wandering session. Collect as many sounds as possible.

WANDERING DRAWINGS

What if the earth retained memories of everything that occurred in specific places? That would mean it might be possible to sit in a place and sense those memories.

Sit in a place for a while. Draw whatever comes into your head.

TIME LOG

Document where you are every ten minutes in your wandering. You may also create a map to plot out your movement.

PERCEPTION HACKING

There are a variety of things we can do to alter our perception of a place or an experience.

- Literally shift your perspective. Look at the same thing from a different viewpoint: hang upside down, get down low, climb up high.

- Play a soundtrack; music alters our experience and shifts moods.

- Framing or blocking out parts of our view allows us to focus on a specific part in a different way.

- Pretend you are a character, either from fiction or from your own imagination. What would that character do? How would they approach the world differently from you? Maybe they would try something that you wouldn't (more daring, more slowly). Wander through various places as this character. How would they approach an art museum? A café?

DOCUMENT THE WIND

Spend a wandering session focusing on movement caused by wind. It would be best to do this on a day where it was at least slightly windy. Document everything you find (photo or video).

FIND THE SLANT OF LIGHT

There's a certain Slant of light, Winter
Afternoons

—EMILY DICKINSON

Spend a wandering session focusing on the quality of light. Document it only if you feel moved to do so.

FIND SOMETHING THAT HAS BEEN TRANSFORMED

Today's wandering is a detective hunt of sorts. You are to go out in search of something that has been transformed and document it in your preferred method. It matters not how it has been transformed; it is up to you to determine how this concept is interpreted.

My words itch at your ears
until you understand them.
-Walt Whitman

HUNT FOR WATER/MOISTURE

Seek out a body of water. It matters not what form this water takes, but you are to seek it nonetheless. If you are in an arid climate, such as the desert, and there is no water in sight, then you shall seek out moisture in an alternative form, whatever that may be. You should spend time examining this water, what is happening around the water, what grows near the water, who uses the water. Take notes.

_____

TINDLEBAUM HAS MADE A NEW DISCOVERY. ACTUALLY THE DISCOVERY CAME TO HIM VIA AN ANONYMOUS SOURCE. IT SEEMS THAT THERE IS A WANDER SOCIETY TWITTER FEED: TWITTER.COM/ZENMASTER782. BUT THE TWEETS SEEM TO INCLUDE SOME KIND OF CODE. THE QUESTION IS, HOW DO WE DECIPHER THEM? THERE MUST BE A KEY HIDDEN SOMEWHERE.

ONE THING

Document one chosen common thing everywhere you go. Some examples: a shape, a color, typography, sewer covers, walls, signs.

SAME AND DIFFERENT

Walk the same route on purpose, noticing different things every time.

Walk different routes on purpose.

dérive
| deRiv | noun
an unplanned journey with the goal of encountering a
new experience. (See page 46.)

THE WANDER SOCIETY

Rivers know this: there is no hurry. We shall get there some day.
--A. A. MILNE, WINNIE-THE-POOH

PSYCHOGEOGRAPHY

The term *psychogeography* refers to the act of exploring a city (usually an urban endeavor) in a nontraditional way. We can choose to explore in ways that incorporate randomness and spontaneity, and in doing so we may transform our familiar streets into something unexpected.

> Psychogeography seeks to overcome the processes of "banalisation" by which the everyday experience of our surroundings becomes one of drab monotony.
>
> —MERLIN COVERLEY, PSYCHOGEOGRAPHY

Remap the city you live in. Create a new experience of it for yourself.

Some ideas for you to start with:

1. Take a map of your town.
2. Place a small cup on the map and draw a circle.
3. Go explore that area fully.

TINDLEBAUM HAS ALSO LOCATED A BUNCH OF WANDER SOCIETY MEMBER ART ON VARIOUS SOCIAL MEDIA. IT SEEMS TWS USES TECHNOLOGY TO SERVE THEIR OWN PURPOSES, AND IN WAYS THAT SUIT THEM, PUTTING THE POWER OF TECHNOLOGY BACK INTO THE HANDS OF THE USER. WE CAN USE IT IN WAYS THAT SERVE OUR CAUSE, NOT IN THE WAYS THAT SOCIETY DICTATES.

Or:

1. Assign a bunch of variables to a die. For example, 1=left, 2=right, 3=forward, 4=pause and look, 5=reverse, 6=you choose.
2. Roll the die at each intersection to determine the direction to travel in.

LEAVE BEHINDS

As part of our wandering mission, you are instructed to subversively plant things in the real world for others to find. It is our hope that in encouraging others to wander through discovery, we can change the world. It can be quite exciting to do this on a regular basis knowing that you may never know who will find them.

Some ideas of things to leave:

- Quotes on paper (see page 161)
- Stickers at the back of this book
- Origami
- Wandering literature (see "How and Why to Make a Wander Society Station" on page 153)
- Seeds and seed bombs
- Stone piles and arrangements
- Found objects
- Small notes

Places to leave things:

- In trees
- In books
- In the woods

THE DISCOVERY OF THE TWITTER FEED HAS IGNITED MY
IMAGINATION. I HAVE NEVER USED TWITTER BEFORE BECAUSE
I FOUND IT MOSTLY UNINTERESTING. BUT WHAT IF IT IS
SECRETLY DELIVERING INFORMATION? I AM DETERMINED
TO CRACK THE CODE.

LEAVING SYMBOLS

Draw some of the symbols and slogans of the Wander Society as you wander. See the "Wander Symbols Key" on page 172.

Ideas for drawing methods: stone piles, drawing in mud, stickers, leaves, chalk.

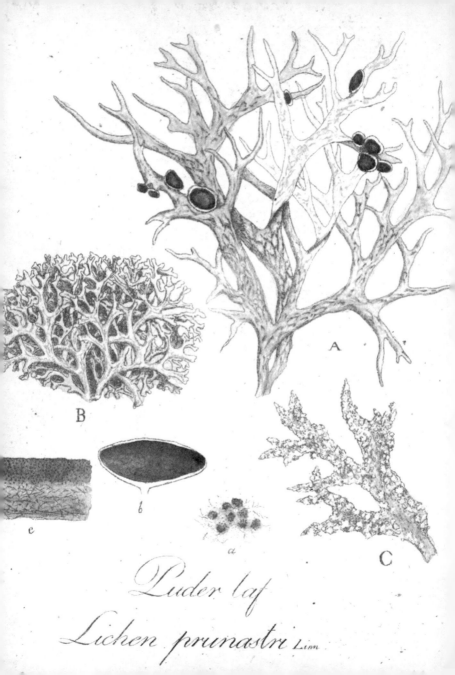

Puder laf

Lichen prunastri Linn.

WANDERING BY BICYCLE

It is possible to practice the wandering mindset while traveling by bicycle. The bicycle can be beneficial as it allows us to cover greater distances and explore more distant territory.

Some tips for traveling by bicycle:

- Racks work best for carrying stuff; backpacks are top-heavy and not recommended.
- With the ability to carry gear, you can easily add some more nomadic accessories (such as a portable tea brewing system, wild food collection system, portable napping system, portable library).
- Always carry tools for fixing a flat, or changing the height of your seat, etc.

During your wandering by bicycle select a destination to partake in a tea ceremony, a nap, or a reading session. Document the experience.

BACK TO WANDERING! I AM LOSING SIGHT OF THE TRUE IMPORTANCE OF THIS SOCIETY. THE REAL WORK. THE IMPORTANT WORK. I AM WAKING UP. AGAIN.

SEEK OUT SPIRITS
HIDING IN PLAIN SIGHT

Many older cultures believe that everything is alive and animate, even apparently inanimate things. This is your chance to give new life to your environment by giving names and personalities to a variety of things: large trees, rocks, creeks, nooks, routes, the wind, plants, hills, landmarks. You are now in charge of renaming everything. Make it your own.

Draw a map with your newly named landmarks.

HOW TO INCORPORATE RANDOMNESS

Flip randomly to a page in this section. Follow the instructions.

Find a local paper. Go to the section that details local happenings and events. Drop a coin onto the page. Go to that event.

On a windy day, follow a leaf that blows wherever it goes.

Ask a friend to give you wandering instructions. Tell your friend to write a location in your journal. Do not look at it until you are ready to set out.

Write a list of places you would like to explore on a piece of paper. Cut them out. Pick one out of a hat.

THE WANDERING REMINDS ME OF WHY I AM HERE. I AM HERE TO EXPERIENCE IT ALL. TO AWAKEN TO IT ALL. TO BE IN THIS BODY. RIGHT HERE. (I FEEL LIKE YELLING.)

IMAGINARY WANDERING

You can also wander new, undiscovered worlds through your imagination via literature. Bring a book with you as you wander and find a quiet corner to read in.

You might choose a book based on

- location. (Do you know you can travel the entire planet through fiction?) Choose a book based on a place you want to visit. It might help to visit a bookstore and talk to the staff for this purpose.
- an imaginary place (you might try science fiction for this).
- a fellow wanderer (see list on page 38).

Some examples of destinations:

Morocco—Paul Bowles, *The Sheltering Sky*
India—Arundhati Roy, *The God of Small Things*
Spain—Hemingway, *The Sun Also Rises; For Whom the Bell Tolls*
England—Daphne Du Marier, *Rebecca*
United States—Kerouac, *On the Road*
Afghanistan—Khaled Hosseini, *The Kite Runner*
Russia—Fyodor Dostoyevsky, *Crime and Punishment*
Italy—Thomas Mann, *Death in Venice*
Japan—Banana Yoshimoto, *Kitchen*
Colombia—Gabriel Garcia Marquez, *One Hundred Years of Solitude*
Canada (Newfoundland)—Annie Proulx, *The Shipping News*

THE ART OF GETTING LOST

While it is not important to get truly lost to complete this assignment, it is beneficial is to visit places in your local environment that you have never been. Look at a map of your city or town. Determine what areas you have not explored. Make a list and tackle them one by one. Occasionally these are places that are difficult to access. Do not let that intimidate you. See if they change your wandering outlook. Leave your mark in these new places.

WAS JUST REMINDED OF A GREAT RITUAL THAT IS PERFECT FOR WANDERING. THINK OF A PAINFUL OR CHALLENGING EXPERIENCE THAT YOU WISH TO RELEASE. FIND A ROCK. PUT THE ENERGY OF THAT EXPERIENCE ONTO THE ROCK. AS YOU THROW THE ROCK, YELL AS LOUDLY AS YOU CAN.

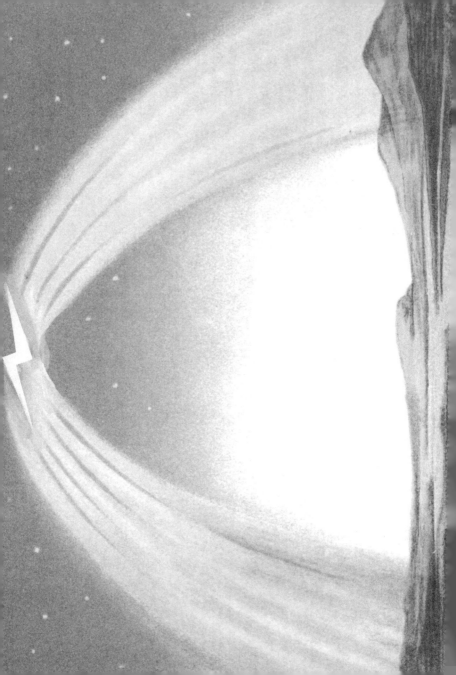

CREATE A
TEMENOS

A temenos is a sacred spot that acts as a space or "safe spot" for mental work to take place.

This can be useful when you are working on a specific project, or if you are just in need of some deep contemplation or meditation.

During your wanderings keep an eye out for a spot that has a good energy to it. You might feel a "pull" to spend time there. Near a body of water is optimal (but not necessary).

To ritualize the experience, when you find your spot you should mark it somehow, possibly with a wander symbol or a stone pile (it does not have to be visible). Only you need to know about it.

LIBRARY WANDERING

You are invited to enter a library with no idea about what to look for, and no attachment to outcome. You are instructed to wander through the shelves choosing books at random that you find interesting.

SOME WAYS TO SUBVERT YOUR BROWSING

Find a book that interests you, and leave it on the shelves. Count seven books down from that one. Read that book.

Locate the first five blue books you see. Take those to a reading chair.

Find a favorite book of yours. Look in the bibliography. Pick a book listed there. Find that book and read it.

Ask the librarian what his or her favorite book is. Locate it and read it.

Find an author with the same last name as you. Read the book. (If you can't find one, locate the closest name to it.)

BEGAN LEAVING TINY QUOTES IN PUBLIC. I FIND IT COMPLETELY ADDICTIVE. THE FIRST ONE I PLACED IN A WALT WHITMAN BOOK AT MY FAVORITE BOOKSTORE. "IT IS OUR HABIT TO THINK OUTDOORS — WALKING, LEAPING, CLIMBING, DANCING, PREFERABLY ON LONELY MOUNTAINS OR NEAR THE SEA WHERE EVEN THE TRAILS BECOME THOUGHTFUL." — FRIEDRICH NIETZSCHE

RANDOM PAINTING

Bring a brush and some water with you on a wandering. See how many things you can use as pigment on your travels: plants, crushed flowers, dirt, coffee, tea, grass, etc.

OUTDOOR STUDIO: TINKERING WITH THINGS/ FOUND MATERIALS

Collect some items while wandering (plants, stones, found objects). Organize them into interesting configurations. Combine them to create new objects. Tinker. Pretend you have a nomadic studio. Everywhere holds the possibility for new creations.

> *A conversation between Andre Breton and Alberto Giacometti:*
> *"What is your studio?" Breton asked.*
> *Giacometti replied: "It is two feet that walk."*
>
> —JAMES LORD, GIACOMETTI: A BIOGRAPHY

LISTENING WHILE WANDERING

When you wander while listening to a particularly good audio book, you mark the landscape with the experiences in the book. Places become inextricably linked to plot points and language. The experience creates a very personal and physical connection to a place. You can "mark" the corners of your town with a story of your choosing. It is most beneficial to choose a book that has deep meaning to you. You may have to listen to the book in segments depending on its length.

FEELING LIKE I AM IN THE CENTER OF A GAME. LOOKING AT PEOPLE ON THE STREET AND WONDERING IF THEY ARE IN THE WANDER SOCIETY.

FOLLOWING/
TRACKING

What can we follow? A path. An animal. A route. A person. A sound. A leaf that blows.

Read "Secrecy, or How to Be Invisible" on page 63. Set out. If you are noticed, abort assignment immediately.

THE QUEST OF THE
RAMBLING WANDERER

This is the ultimate mission for you, dear Wander Society member.

This wander will be more involved wandering than you have ever done. The exact form of the wandering cannot be written here, in part because it is secret, and in part because it is to be determined by you. However, know that it will be your greatest wandering ever, to be completed only after you have become a seasoned wanderer. The purpose of this mission is to solidify your commitment to the wandering path and to celebrate your achievements as a wanderer.

You must not take this task lightly. It will signify a great turning point in your journey, in the form of a deepening relationship with the self. This will be apparent by a change in your outlook, a belief in the sacred nature of your wanderings, and a deeply felt connection with the place in which you wander.

THE MORE WE LIVE BY OUR INTELLECT, THE LESS WE UNDERSTAND THE MEANING OF LIFE. — LEO TOLSTOY

You will now devise a new wandering for yourself. This one will be longer than you have ever done before.

It should be something that you are not sure if you can do, that is to say, it should scare you a little. You should incorporate some of your passions and favorite activities. Some examples:

- A trip to a place you've never been
- Embarking on a project you've always wanted to do but were too scared to attempt
- A pilgrimage to a sacred place (the resting place of your favorite author)
- A crazy random adventure devised by you

CAME TO THE REALIZATION THAT TWS WORKS FOR ME BECAUSE I AM VERY INTROVERTED. I LOVE THAT THERE IS NO PRESSURE TO INTERACT WITH OTHER PEOPLE YET I AM STILL PARTICIPATING IN A GROUP ACTIVITY. SIMILAR IN CONCEPT TO RADIO (IN REAL TIME). I HAVE OFTEN THOUGHT ABOUT THIS IN THE CONTEXT OF MY OWN BOOKS (WRECK). MY YOUNGER TEENAGE SELF WOULD HAVE LOVED TO PARTICIPATE IN SOME KIND OF NON-MEETING COMMUNITY.

WE ARE INFINITE

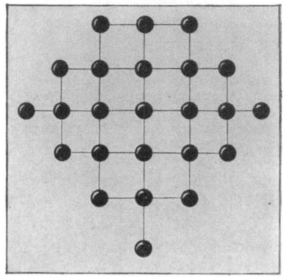

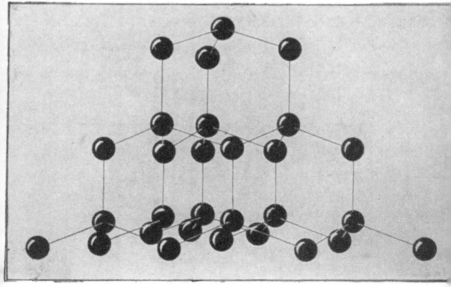

HOW-TO SECTION

What if our life skills had more value than our worldly possessions? The most content human by far is one who can create a world out of nothing.

—UNKNOWN WANDER SOCIETY MEMBER

WHO ARE WE IF WE LEAVE OUR COMMUNITY BEHIND? WHO ARE WE WITHOUT ALL OF OUR STORIES? WITHOUT ALL OF OUR STUFF? WHO WOULD YOU BE IF YOU COULD BEGIN AGAIN?

HOW TO MAKE A
WANDER BADGE

You will need:

- Some kind of thick fabric; waxed canvas, wool felt, or plain canvas work well (if you only have thin fabric, you can still make this using an embroidery hoop to stretch the fabric)
- Chalk or marking pencil
- Small ring
- Embroidery thread in one or two different colors
- Embroidery needle
- Scissors
- Fray stop or white glue

1. Trace a large circle onto the fabric using the chalk or marking pencil.

2. Trace both the inside and the outside of a small ring inside the larger circle.

3. Draw a lightning bolt in the middle.

4. Stitch the lightning bolt using split stitch. (Sewing techniques at thewandersociety.com)

5. Stitch the ring in the color of your choice using satin stitch. (Sewing techniques at thewandersociety.com)

6. Finish edges with fray stop or white glue to prevent fraying.

7. Sew to item of your choice.

RAN DOWN A LONG HILL SCREAMING AND JUMPING.
FEELING MORE ALIVE THAN I HAVE IN A LONG TIME.
SOLVITUR AMBULANDO! I HAVE LEFT BEHIND THE
SHACKLES OF CONVENTION. I HAVE DONE THIS BEFORE
BUT I OFTEN FORGET THAT I SHOULD.

HOW TO CARVE A
WANDERING STICK

You will need:

- A tree branch
- A small saw
- A pocket knife
- Sandpaper (optional)

1. Go on a hunt for a stick that is 1½ to 2 inches in diameter. You can use dead wood (wood that has fallen from a tree), but it will be harder to carve and possibly lacking in strength. Green wood from a newly fallen branch of a leafy tree is easier to carve and will have greater strength. Avoid cutting from a live tree if possible. Wanderers try to cause the least harm to their environment.

2. Use the saw to cut the branch to a length that feels good to you (approximately 6 inches above your elbow).

HAD AN INTERESTING REVELATION TODAY WHILE WANDERING. I AM NO LONGER OBSESSED WITH "WHO IS" THE WANDER SOCIETY. IT SEEMS MORE IMPORTANT TO CONTINUE THE WORK FOR MYSELF. I AM TWS. HA HA! (STILL TRYING TO CRACK THE CODE THOUGH.)

3. Using your pocket knife, whittle the bark from the stick, making sure to slide the knife away from you as you slice. You may wish to carve one of the symbols of the Wander Society at the top of your stick or use sandpaper to smooth any rough edges. Your wandering stick will darken as it dries.

HOW TO KNIT A
WRIST CUFF

This project may require some previous knitting experience. If you are familiar with the seed stitch you will have no problem. You may also use this as an opportunity (read: challenge) to learn something you have never done before.

You will need:

- Cloth tape measure or ruler
- Pencil
- Yarn (we used sock-weight here)
- Knitting needles
- Yarn needle
- Button
- Scissors
- Fabric for pocket at least 3½-by-2 inches (optional; you can also knit the pocket)
- Iron
- Hand-sewing needle (for cloth pocket version)
- Thread (for cloth pocket version)

1. Measure your wrist with a cloth tape measure, or wrap a piece of yarn around wrist and measure it on a flat ruler.

2. Knit a gauge swatch. Follow the instructions on the yarn label or cast on 20 to 25 stitches and knit in seed stitch (alternating knit, purl) for 20 to 25 rows or until the piece measures approximately 4 inches. Count the number of stitches and the number of rows in 1 square inch and write down these numbers.

3. Determine the size of your wristband. The measurement of your wrist plus 2 inches for overlap by 1½ to 2 inches wide. Multiply the number of stitches and rows per inch to determine how many stitches to cast on and how many rows to knit. You can knit the wristband lengthwise or widthwise.

4. Knit the wristband.

Knitting Lengthwise

Cast on determined number of stitches and knit in seed stitch until you have 1 inch left to knit. The buttonhole should be 2 or 3 stitches wide, depending on the size of your button—determine the center of your wristband and knit to 1 or 2 stitches away from that center, depending on whether you are making a 2-stitch buttonhole or a 3-stitch buttonhole. To make the buttonhole: Bring yarn forward and slip the first stitch on the left needle purlwise. Bring the yarn to the back. Slip the next stitch on the left needle purlwise to the right needle. Pass the second slipped stitch on the right needle over the first stitch (as if to bind off). Repeat until the buttonhole is the right size. Slip the last bound-off stitch to the left needle. Turn the work and use the backward loop to cast on 1 more stitch than you bound off. Turn the work. Slip the first stitch on the left needle to the right needle and pass the extra cast-on stitch over the slipped stitch. Work the remaining stitches on the needle. Continue knitting for 1 more inch, when your wristband should measure the size of your wrist plus 2 inches and cast off. Using the yarn needle, sew in the ends. Sew the button on the center of the wristband, 1 inch from the end, opposite the end with the buttonhole.

DO YOU EVER JUST FEEL LIKE YOU COULD CHANGE THE WORLD IF YOU WERE GIVEN THE VOICE? IN THE WORLD OF TWS IT FEELS A BIT LIKE YOU HAVE BEEN GIVEN A VOICE. BUT IT'S UP TO YOU TO PUT IT OUT THERE. IT FEELS LIKE I HAVE MORE CREATIVE CONTROL THAN I THOUGHT. AND THE POWER TO AFFECT OTHERS. EXCEPT NOBODY KNOWS IT'S YOU. I CAN LITERALLY PAINT MY TOWN WITH IDEAS.

Knitting Widthwise

Cast on determined number of stitches and knit in seed stitch until you have knit half of the wristband. On one end, knit for 1 inch and then make the buttonhole (see instructions on previous page). Continue knitting the second half of the wristband and cast off and sew in the ends with the yarn needle. Sew the button on the center of the wristband, 1 inch from the end, opposite the end with the buttonhole.

5. Make the pocket. Cut a piece of cloth that measures 3½ inches wide by 2 inches tall. Fold down and press with an iron ¼ inch on each side and bottom of pocket. Fold the top of the pocket down another ¼ inch and whipstitch. Using whipstitch again, sew the pocket to the underside of the wristband and sew along sides and bottom to form pocket.

To Knit the Pocket

Using your gauge, knit in seed stitch a 3-inch wide by 1¼-inch tall rectangle, and sew onto the underside of the wristband.

SPENT SOME TIME DOCUMENTING SOUNDS. WAS AMAZED BY MAGNITUDE I EXPERIENCED IN THE SPAN OF ONE HOUR! THE WORLD GROWS MORE EXPANSIVE.

HOW TO SEW A
NECK POUCH

A neck pouch is the perfect way to carry quotes with you at all times. Just wearing it will make you feel immensely powerful and capable of great things.

You will need:

- Medium-weight fabric in one color (old clothes, such as jeans, are good for this)
- Strong string or leather lace
- A button or sew-on snap closure
- Needle and thread
- Embroidery thread (optional)
- Iron

1. Cut out a rectangle of cloth measuring 7-by-2½ inches.

2. Fold down ¼ inch on all edges. Press with an iron and baste.

3. Fold bottom of pouch up 2½ inches and sew sides.

4. Braid yarn into cord for strap, if desired, and knot ends to keep from unraveling. Sew braided strap onto underside of flap, above pouch opening.

5. Add a button to front of the pouch and a loop to the top of flap as shown in the photo on page 143.

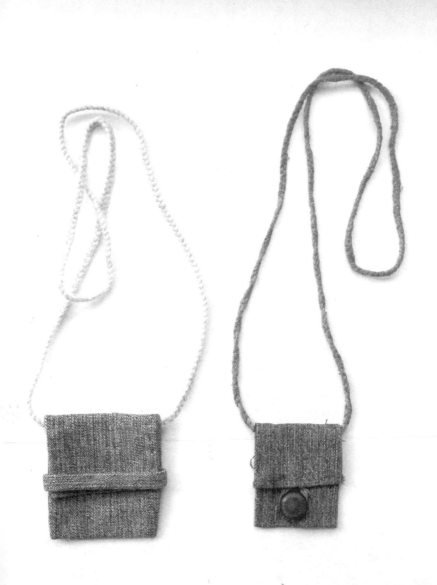

HOW TO MAKE A
WANDER BELT POUCH

You will need:

- Scissors
- Piece of waxed canvas measuring at least 7-by-10½ inches
- Piece of cloth for lining flap measuring at least 9½-by-5 inches (optional, can use waxed canvas)
- Piece of waxed canvas measuring 3-by-5 inches for the strap
- Iron
- Sewing machine (or can be hand-sewn)
- Sewing thread
- Hand-sewing needle
- Heavy paper or cardboard for corner template
- Pencil
- Ruler
- Embroidery floss or heavy-weight thread for buttonhole (optional)
- Button

I'VE BEEN THINKING A LOT LATELY ABOUT HOW, WITH ITS FOCUS ON PRODUCTIVITY, SOCIETY DOESN'T ALLOW FOR UNPLANNED TIME AND PURSUITS LIKE WANDERING, AS THEY FALL UNDER THE CATEGORY OF IDLENESS. WE ARE TAUGHT TO EXPERIENCE FEELINGS OF GUILT AND SHAME WHEN WE ARE NOT ACTIVELY DOING SOMETHING PRODUCTIVE (WASTING TIME). BUT WHAT IF WANDERING IS THE REAL WORK? IN NOURISHING OUR BODIES GIVING SPACE FOR OUR MINDS AND HEARTS TO BREATHE, CARING FOR THE SOUL, AND LETTING THE SUBCONSCIOUS MIND TACKLE PROBLEMS, WE ARE ACTUALLY DOING MUCH MORE FOR OURSELVES AND THE WORLD. THIS IS THE BIG WORK.

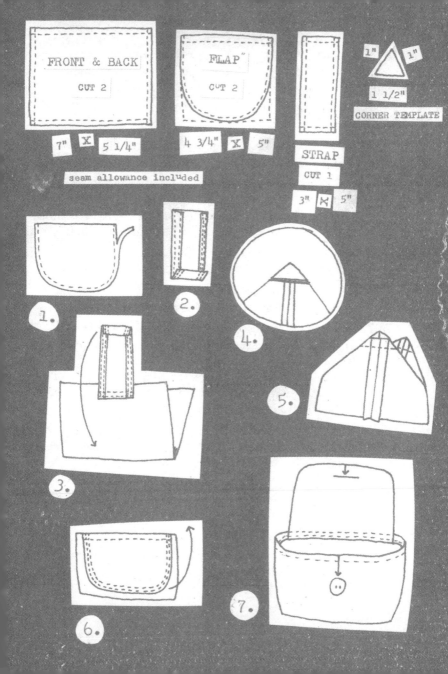

FRONT & BACK

CUT 2

FLAP

CUT 2

7" X 5 1/4"   4 3/4" X 5"

seam allowance included

1"   1"

1 1/2"

CORNER TEMPLATE

STRAP

CUT 1

3" X 5"

1.

2.

3.

4.

5.

6.

7.

1. Cut all the pattern pieces out of the waxed canvas and a piece of cloth for the lining using the measurements provided.

2. Using a round object, trace round corners on the flap pieces.

3. Zigzag (sewing machine) or overcast stitch (hand-sewing) around the edges of each piece to prevent fraying.

4. Layer flap pieces with right sides together and stitch around sides and bottom of flap using a ¼-inch seam allowance. Trim seam allowance to ⅛ inch after stitching **(figure 1)**. Turn right side out and iron flat. Topstitch.

5. With right sides together, stitch front to back along the bottom seam using a ½-inch seam allowance.

6. Fold under ½ inch on the long edges and topstitch. Fold up one short edge of the strap ½ inch **(figure 2)**.

7. Matching the center of the strap with the center of the back of the pouch, stitch unfolded edge of the strap to the pouch ¾ inch from the top with two rows of stitching **(figure 3)**. Fold down and again, matching the center of the strap with the center of the back of the bag, stitch the bottom of strap ½ inch up from the bottom of the pouch—in a box shape of stitching.

8. With right sides together, stitch up the sides of the pouch using a ½-inch seam allowance.

9. With the pouch inside out, line up the side seam with the bottom seam and trace the bottom edge of the corner template onto the pouch **(figure 4)**; this will be the stitching line.

10. Stitch along the line you made in step 9 **(figure 5)** and turn pouch right side out.

11. With right sides together, line up the center of the flap with the center of the back of the pouch and stitch, using a ½-inch seam allowance **(figure 6)**.

12. Iron flap up and press remaining ½-inch seam allowance on the top edge of the pouch to the inside. Topstitch around the top.

13. Make the buttonhole by measuring ¾ inch up from the bottom of the flap **(figure 7)** and drawing a line that matches the width of your button. Cut along this line and overcast stitch around the edges with embroidery floss or heavy thread.

14. Measure 2 inches down from the top of the front **(figure 7)** and sew a button here.

BEGAN SEWING SOME WS PARAPHERNALIA.

HOW TO MAKE A
WANDERING NOTEBOOK

There is a long tradition of wanderers making their own note-books. Many great writers like Mary Oliver, Kim Stafford, and Walt Whitman preferred to make their own small hand-sewn versions rather than use something store-bought. These compact books fit into a pouch or pocket for easy access while wandering.

Almost all [of Whitman's] writing was done with a pencil in a sort of loose book that he carried in his breast pocket. The book consisted of a few sheets of good white paper, folded and fastened with a pin or two. He said he had tried all sorts of note-books and he liked that kind best.

—RICHARD BUCKE, COSMIC CONSCIOUSNESS

WHY DO WE ALWAYS FEEL THE NEED TO BUY EVERYTHING? SURELY WE ARE MORE RESOURCEFUL THAN THAT? SOMETHING TO THINK ABOUT.

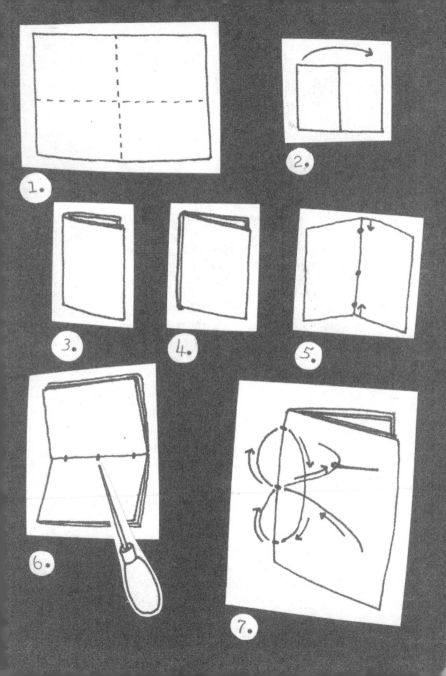

1.

2.

3.

4.

5.

6.

7.

You will need:

- Knife or scissors
- 3 sheets of 8½-by-11-inch paper for a 24-page book*
- 1 piece of heavy paper at least 6-by-4¼ inches for the cover
- Pencil
- Ruler
- 2 large paper clips or binding clips (optional)
- Push pin or awl
- Heavy-weight thread or yarn or embroidery floss or string or dental floss for binding (at least 12 inches long)
- Sewing needle with an eye large enough to accommodate the thread/string you are using

1. Cut or tear each sheet of paper in half into 4¼-by-11-inch pieces of paper. Cut or tear each of those pieces in half into 4¼-by-5½-inch pieces **(figure 1)**. Fold each of those pieces of paper in half to create the pages of the notebook; they should measure 2¾ inches wide by 4¼ inches tall **(figure 2)**.

2. Sandwich all pages inside of each other like a book **(figure 3)**.

3. Cut a piece of heavy paper for the cover that measures 6-by-4¼ inches. Fold in half into a 3-inch wide by 4¼-inch tall cover. Place the cover around the outside of the pages. **(figure 4)**.

4. Remove the center page and fold it in half lengthwise to crease-mark the center of the spine. With a pencil, make a dot at this crease. Measure ¾ inch down on the spine from the top of the book and make a pencil dot; measure ¾ inch up on the spine from the bottom of the book and make another pencil dot **(figure 5)**. Place this page back in the center of your book; this will be your binding template.

5. Line up all pages and cover (tap book against a hard surface—like a table—to align the pages, if needed) and use paper clips or binding clips to hold pages and cover together (optional). Using the push pin or awl, push holes through all pages and cover on the spine at the three spots marked with a pencil from step 5 **(figure 6)**.

6. Thread the needle and double the thread if it is thin—no need to make a knot. Decide if you want to tie off your notebook on the outside or inside.

Sewing Instructions for Tying Off Notebook on Outside

Begin on the outside of the notebook and go into the center hole, leaving a 2- to 3-inch tail of thread on the outside of the notebook. Come back to the outside of the spine through either hole near the top or bottom of the notebook, go back into the notebook at the other hole that hasn't been used yet, and come back out the center hole. With two square knots, tie off the thread and trim it to desired length.

WAS IN MY LOCAL BOOKSTORE BUYING A COPY OF
BECOMING ANIMAL BY DAVID ABRAM FOR MY RESEARCH.
THE CLERK POINTED ME TO A COPY OF TWS INTRO
PAMPHLET AND ASKED ME IF I WROTE IT. I SAID,
"NO, WHY DO YOU ASK?" SHE TOLD ME THAT SOMEONE HAD
BEEN SENDING THEM TO THE STORE AND THEY WERE
TRYING TO FIGURE OUT WHO IT WAS. I EXPLAINED THAT
I HAVE BEEN ON A SIMILAR PATH OF LATE.

Sewing Instructions for Tying Off Notebook on Inside

Begin on the inside of the notebook and go out the center hole, leaving a 2- to 3-inch tail of thread on the inside of the notebook. Come back to the inside of the spine through either hole near the top or bottom of the notebook, go back to the outside of the notebook at the other hole that hasn't been used yet, and come back in using the center hole. With two square knots, tie off thread and trim to desired length **(figure 7)**.

*Minimal Notebook

To make a minimal notebook, follow the first two steps on page 150, using a rubber band around the spine to hold the pages together.

- 2 sheets of 8½-by-11-inch paper for a 16-page book
- Rubber band

THE NEXT TIME I WAS IN THE STORE, SHE SHOWED ME THE MOST RECENT MAILING. A NEW ZINE I HADN'T SEEN BEFORE. NO RETURN ADDRESS. I SCOUR IT FOR CLUES.

HOW AND WHY
TO MAKE A
WANDER SOCIETY STATION

As members of the Wander Society, we take on a sense of owner-ship of our environment and the place we live in. In this sense, we become caretakers and stewards of the earth. Once people begin to realize that everything is connected, they begin to act in differ-ent ways. They realize that this planet is a living, breathing thing and if you cause harm to one part of it the consequences are felt by all.

Through nurturing our connection with our immediate envi-ronment, we members of the Wander Society gain a deep, first-hand understanding of the role we all play in the success of the planet. We also foster a belief in using only what we need, what we have around us to create our existence, and we tread lightly. We use the tools of instinct, intuition, and experimentation.

NOTICED THAT ONE OF THE OLDER WANDER
STATIONS HAS BEEN VANDALIZED. MADE ME FEEL
SAD ABOUT THE WORLD. BUT I REMIND MYSELF THAT
THE SPIRIT OF TWS IS INVINCIBLE. IT WILL FIGHT BACK
WITH MORE STATIONS IN NEW LOCATIONS!

We do this first by learning to take care of ourselves and our own needs, giving ourselves space and time to ponder, to daydream. Then, by caring for the needs of our city/village and everything around it, we develop a deep sense of gratitude for the gifts we receive on our wanderings, and a feel for and understanding of the balance of all things. We reawaken a deep love of the earth and turn our wanderings into an art form.

This experience is accessible to all people. Imagine a world where most of us felt this way. Much of the damage and destruction we see today would not exist. It is the wanderer's mission to take what he or she has learned and pass it on to others. It is our way of giving back and reawakening this deep love in others. In this way, it is possible to foster a movement that promotes a deep awareness of ourselves and a harmony with nature.

You can help create this movement by putting up Wander Society stations in your city or town. These stations hold small pamphlets that you can print out and fold and leave in secret places for others to find.

You will need:

- Computer and printer
- Scissors
- Cardboard
- Marker
- Utility knife
- Glue
- String or ribbon
- Packing tape or clear acrylic sealer (Mod Podge or something similar)

I SHOWED THE BOOKSTORE CLERK SOME OF MY WS ARTIFACTS AND TOLD HER ABOUT THE TINDLEBAUM WEBSITE. SHE SEEMED TO BE QUITE EXCITED. I THINK TWS MIGHT HAVE A NEW RECRUIT.

1. Print out the station template found at thewandersociety
.com/station_instructions.pdf or use template on page 157.

2. Cut it out and trace it onto cardboard with a marker.

3. Using a utility knife, cut out the cardboard station.

4. Score on the lines and cut the slots as indicated on the template.

5. Fold and insert the sides through the slots.

6. Glue or draw a "Take One" sign to the front of the station.

7. Thread some string or ribbon through the back slots.

8. For a bit of weatherproofing, you may wish to cover the
station with clear packing tape or some clear acrylic sealer
such as Mod Podge (stay away from aerosols as they are
harmful to the environment).

9. Print out several pamphlets found at thewandersociety
.com/intro_pam_instr.pdf and fold according to these
instructions (see pdf illustration).

10. Place the pamphlets in the station and head out.

11. Tie the station to trees or other spots you find suitable.
(Choose locations that are somewhat weatherproof so that
the station will last as long as possible.) The station will
deteriorate naturally over time. This is okay. Nothing in life
is permanent.

12. Check on your stations periodically to see if they need more
pamphlets. Don't worry if they have been vandalized or
stolen. People realize their power and sometimes want to
use it to sabotage. Just make another station and change
locations.

THE BOOKSTORE CALLED ME OVER THE WEEKEND
TO TELL ME THAT A STENCIL OF WHITMAN HAD
APPEARED ONE MORNING ON THEIR SIDEWALK.

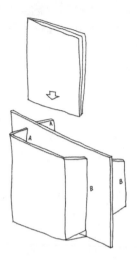

WANDER STATION INSTRUCTIONS

1. Print and cut out template.
2. Trace onto cardboard. Cut out.
3. Score and fold along dotted lines.
4. Tuck side A into slot A.
5. Tuck side B into slot B.
6. Add logo and the words "Take One" to the front of the station. You may also wish to weatherproof the cardboard slightly by adding some packing tape to cover the station.

7. Slide ribbon or string through slot C & D.

8. Print and fold pamphlets from thewandersociety.com or make your own.

9. Insert pamphlets. Tie to a tree or post.

TAKE ONE

Enlarge image to 200% before tracing onto cardboard.

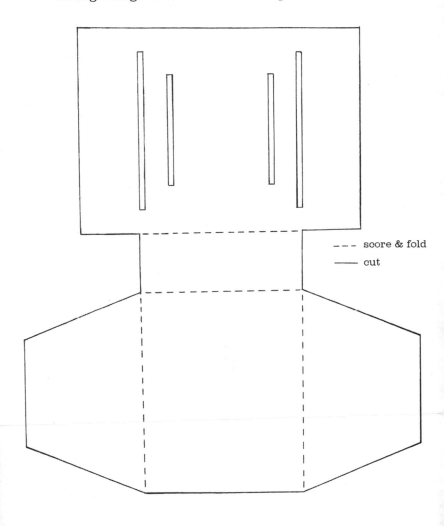

- - - score & fold
—— cut

USEFUL KNOTS

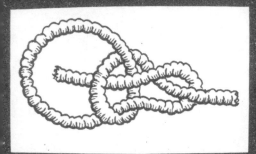

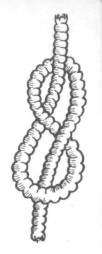

BOWLINE or "King of Knots"
- makes a loop at the end of
a rope, the knot is strong
under tension and is easy to
untie in different types
of weather.

FIGURE OF EIGHT KNOT
- useful for preventing
the end of a piece of rope
from fraying, this knot
is easier to untie than the
overhand knot.

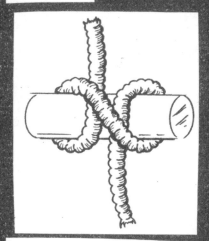

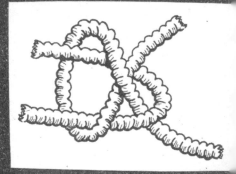

CLOVE HITCH
- use this to quickly attach
the end of a length of rope
to an object. This knot may loosen
under diagonal tension, but not
under perpendicular tension.

SHEET BEND
- a bend ties two ropes
together, the sheet bend is
helpful when joining two
ropes of differing thickness
and type. If a rope is too
short, use the sheet bend
to add another piece.

WANDER SOCIETY LEXICON

Activator: Member of the Wander Society who identifies a need in his or her community and uses WS methods to solve it.

Annotation: The act of writing in the margins of books as a form of guerrilla art.

Debugging: The act of going on a wander with the purpose of shifting one's mental state. Usually employed after using too much technology.

Grazing: Sitting in a contemplative fashion.

Harvesting: Collecting artifacts. Sometimes referred to as foraging.

Mind viewing: Meditation.

Offering: The ritualistic act of leaving an object in a public place with the intent of releasing stagnant energy.

Openhearted: Living in an awake manner, accessing a higher level of consciousness.

Oracle: Text from the writings of wanderers.

Querying: Asking fellow wanderers for insight and guidance.

Seeding: The act of putting guerrilla art out into the world.

The Sleepers: Non Wander Society members.

Station drop: The act of leaving a wander station in a public location.

Tracking: Going on a pilgrimage to important sites of wanderers.

Vortals: Sacred landmarks of wanderers.

Wander cache: A gathering of members in a public location with the purpose of performing a specific task. Also referred to as "the gathering."

to wander is to be awakened.

LEAVE BEHIND QUOTES

Cut out or copy any of these that speak to you and leave them in various places on your wanderings. Sharing the wandering philosophy is our way of giving back and hopefully awakening a similar passion in others.

As art cannot be taught and there are no human teachers, there are only two teachers, if you want a teacher at all: one is your own childhood, your own self; the other is nature.

—*FRIEDENSREICH HUNDERTWASSER*

Each of us inevitable; Each of us limitless—each of us with his or her right upon the earth.

—*WALT WHITMAN, "SALUT AU MONDE"*

Methinks that the moment my legs begin to move, my thoughts begin to flow.

—*HENRY DAVID THOREAU, 1851 JOURNAL ENTRY*

I HAVE BECOME AWARE OF THE FACT THAT THIS JOURNEY CAME TO ME AT THE PERFECT TIME. I HAD BEEN NEEDING SOMETHING TO HELP SHAKE ME OUT OF A RUT, TO WAKE ME UP A BIT.

When I go out of the house for a walk, uncertain as yet whither I will bend my steps, and submit myself to my instinct to decide for me, I find, strange and whimsical as it may seem, that I finally and inevitably settle southwest, toward some particular wood or meadow or deserted pasture or hill in that direction.

—HENRY DAVID THOREAU, WALKING

It is not down in any map; true places never are.

—HERMAN MELVILLE, MOBY-DICK

Never trust any thought you have while sitting down.

—FRIEDRICH NIETZSCHE

Go to the pine if you want to learn about pine, or to the bamboo if you want to learn about bamboo. And in doing so, you must leave your subjective preoccupation with yourself.

—BASHŌ

THE LINE BETWEEN INVESTIGATING/BEING A FOLLOWER OF TWS AND BEING A MEMBER SEEMS TO NO LONGER EXIST. I FEEL COMPELLED TO SEND OUT THE MESSAGES OF THE GROUP. THE WORLD NEEDS IT. I AM ENJOYING THE MYSTERY OF IT ALL.

Getting and spending, we lay waste our powers:
Little we see in Nature that is ours.

> —WILLIAM WORDSWORTH

The path is not somewhere in the sky, It is in our hearts.

> —THE BUDDHA

Most of the luxuries and many of the so-called comforts of life are not only not indispensable, but positive hindrances to the elevation of mankind.

> —HENRY DAVID THOREAU, WALDEN

For my part, I travel not to go anywhere, but to travel for travel's sake. The great affair is to move; to feel the needs and hitches of our life more nearly; to come down off this feather-bed of civilization, and find the glove granite underfoot and strewn with cutting flints.

> —ROBERT LOUIS STEVENSON,
> TRAVELS WITH A DONKEY IN THE CEVENNES

DEAR READER, WILL YOU JOIN ME? WHAT WILL YOU SHARE WITH THE WORLD? WILL YOU HONOR YOUR OWN STRENGTHS AND GIFTS AND MAKE A PACT TO EMBODY THE FORCE THAT YOU ARE? WW WILL SHOW YOU THE WAY.

What do you suppose will satisfy the soul except to walk free and own no superior?

—WALT WHITMAN, "LAWS FOR CREATIONS"

This is still the strangest thing in all man's travelling, that he should carry about with him incongruous memories.

—ROBERT LOUIS STEVENSON,
THE SILVERADO SQUATTERS

If one advances confidently in the direction of his dreams, and endeavors to live the life which he has imagined, he will meet with a success unexpected in common hours. . . . In proportion as he simplifies his life, the laws of the universe will appear less complex, and solitude will not be solitude, nor poverty poverty, nor weakness weakness.

—HENRY DAVID THOREAU, WALDEN

HOW MANY MEMBERS ARE ALREADY OUT THERE?
HOW CAN WE INFLUENCE THE WORLD? HOW CAN WE CREATE
MEANING FOR OURSELVES, INSTEAD OF WHAT HAS BEEN
DICTATED TO US? THE NEXT PAGE EXPLAINS IT <u>ALL</u>.
READ ON. MEMORIZE IT IF YOU CAN!

This is what you shall do: Love the earth and sun and the animals, despise riches, give alms to every one that asks, stand up for the stupid and crazy, devote your income and labor to others, hate tyrants, argue not concerning God, have patience and indulgence toward the people, take off your hat to nothing known or unknown or to any man or number of men, go freely with powerful uneducated persons and with the young and with the mothers of families, read these leaves in the open air every season of every year of your life, re-examine all you have been told at school or church or in any book, dismiss whatever insults your own soul, and your very flesh shall be a great poem and have the richest fluency not only in its words but in the silent lines of its lips and face and between the lashes of your eyes and in every motion and joint of your body.

—WALT WHITMAN,
FROM *THE PREFACE* OF LEAVES OF GRASS

WW, YOU HAVE MY HEART.

THE WANDER SOCIETY

THE WANDERER'S CREED

Let us not be tied down by clocks, schedules, rules, dictates. Let us remember who we were before we learned these things. We are the masters of our own existence.

Let us conjure the spirit of Whitman, who roamed the streets of Manhattan, and combed through every tiny seed that sparked his interest. Let us approach the world with the same vigor and intensity.

Let us allow our wild spirits to roam unfettered and unbound. Let us roar and howl and voice our deepest yearnings without caring what others will think about us.

Let us investigate, explore, uncover. Let us follow every lead that we find interesting. There is no limit to our curiosity.

Let us explore our own inner wildness and wander through its tangled brambles. We will emerge knowing that we are stronger and more powerful than we thought.

Let us teach ourselves what we most need to learn. Let us create our own tools and use them in our travels. Let us know deeply that we have everything we need.

Let us remember that things are not what make us fulfilled. Experiences are.

Let us disrupt the everyday banality and reinvent the world in our own image. We are not a target market.

Let us create a bond with the unknown wilderness we are about to enter into even though it might scare us a little.

Let us make peace with our fears and remind ourselves that they hold no power over us. They are just thoughts, not reality (even if it doesn't feel like it sometimes).

Let us come to understand that we are immensely powerful, and that through our wandering we will change the world.

WE WILL CHANGE THE WORLD!

Wander Symbols Key

Wander Station nearby	Wander Society was here	Leave a message
Good wandering place	Go in this direction	Look for surprises
Good wild spot	We are infinite	Enter the unknown
Leave something for me to find	Community of higher consciousness	Seek calm here

*This key was found in a Wander Society zine. It gives us some insight into the symbol interpretation. It seems that the symbols are used to communicate things between members, a form of vernacular. There are some symbols that seem to have no meaning attached. It seems likely that it is up to the members to assign their own meaning to those.

Wander Symbols Key

You are not alone

Wander Society landmark

Bad place to wander

Good listening spot

The answer you seek is here

Wander route is marked

THE PEREGRINATOR

PER-E-GRI-NATE VERB TO WANDER AROUND FROM PLACE TO PLACE. | A WANDER SOCIETY PUBLICATION

HOW TO PLAY TENNIS

This newsletter is not about tennis. This is not to say there is anything wrong with tennis, or the culture surrounding tennis. We here at the Wander Society want to state publicly that the pursuit of tennis as a means of spending time is perfectly valid for a large number of people and that those people are probably quite interesting. We would like to state for the record that we do not play tennis, (with exception of one member, who did play tennis obsessively every day, for a period of less than one year*). That is not to say that we may suddenly decide to start one day, but as of this printing that has not occured.

You are probably thinking right about now, "Well what is this newsletter about if not about tennis?" Surely it could be related to tennis in some way, could it not? The answer to this question is quite a complicated one.   Certainly it would be possible to speak philosophically about tennis and the aims of the tennis player. What goes through the mind of the player as he/she set up a shot?

For the answer to this question we turn our sights to the late and brilliant author David Foster Wallace and his thoughts on basketball.

"The real, many-veiled answer to the question of just what goes through a great player's mind as he stands at the center of hostile crowd-noise and lines up the free-throw that will decide the game might well be: nothing at all."

We at the Wander Society believe that most things in life would benefit from a little more lightheartedness, our full attention in all activities, and solitude (it is not to be feared).

*to our knowledge he has not played tennis since that time, however he does think about playing tennis with some amount of fondness and longing

ODE TO A DUSTY BOOKSHOP

As you enter through the front door a bell rings alerting the proprietor to a new arrival. Often the clerk is off in a back room somewhere or high up on a ladder engaged in the important work of book location, an art that they have been perfecting for the last twenty years or so. They offer you a little nod which says, "I acknowledge your presence but I know that you need some space to peruse the shelves in a solitary fashion. I will be here if and only if you need me. Otherwise you are on your own."

You make your way to a quiet corner, knowing full well this is not the section you are seeking, but the space will give you a few moments to acclimate to the quiet and sink into the energy of the bookstore. You become aware of the smell of old books and run your hands over the spines of the shelf marked 'nature books.'   You make your way to the section marked 'literature', curious if they have a copy of the book you are seeking. This is the book that several people, none of whom know each other, have recommended to you, so you take this as a sign from the universe that this is a book you must read. There is some piece of knowledge in this volume that is to be passed specifically to you. A piece of information that you will need on your quest, because it will help you to move in a new direction. You drop your bag carefully onto the floor and bend down to be closer to the "M" section. You decide it would be best to just get comfortable sitting on the floor while perusing the titles. There is no need to rush this process after all. Books that you are meant to read have a habit of finding you, but only if you give them the space and time to do so. This is a tried and true fact. The book that speaks to you may not be the one you came for. Occasionally it could be the one on the shelf below that reaches out and punches you in the gut.

The bell on the door rings it's somewhat jarring jingle, signaling to the clerk to raise their head and nod their much practiced unobtrusive greeting. You realize now how much you have already become comfortable in your new setting. You pull a book off the shelf and adjust your sitting position, relaxing even more. You open the cover and let your eye move over the page in excited little jumps. The words you are looking for might just be here. Maybe. Time will tell.

There is no need to rush.

The word Wittgenstein used for 'thought', Denkbewegungen, is a coinage that might be translated as "thought movements", 'thought-ways', or 'paths of thought': ideas that have been brought into being by means of motions along a path. -Robert Macfarlane

R'S BROOKLYN STORY

When I reached my destination in Brooklyn, I was hungry and tired, so I sat on some steps across the street from 28 Old Fulton Street and had a snack. After people-watching for about twenty minutes, I saw a man who looked familiar to me, dressed in an overcoat and carrying a red backpack, walking past. I confess I could not place where I had seen him before. Two minutes later he walked by again, this time heading back in the direction he came from. I thought about saying something to him, but at the time I wasn't thinking that this could be connected to TWS in any way. I wish I had.

After I packed up my snack, I headed around the corner to get a better look at the Eagle Warehouse. The building is located on the site of an old newspaper building, where Whitman worked as an editor; it is now a large brown brick warehouse that contains fancy loft condos. On the front of the building, there's a plaque dedicated to Whitman.

As I was studying the building, I noticed there was something tied to the tree next to me. As I went closer I saw that it was a larger version of a Wander Station and inside were several copies of a newspaper called *The Peregrinator, A Wander Society Publication*. I felt my heart flip! My gamble had paid off! I hugged the paper to my chest and felt myself wanting to run excitedly down the street.

Instead of taking the subway back to my friend's studio, I decided to walk for a while. About an hour in, I jolted when I realized that the man I had seen looked remarkably like Nick Papadimitriou, none other than the London Perambulator!

This was the name of a documentary I had watched only a month before on YouTube, about a man who loved to wander the streets of London in search of the places that are discarded or neglected by modern society, places on the margins. Nick is a true wanderer and the inventor of the concept of "deep topography," a practice of listening to, observing, and recording everything in one's immediate landscape. I kicked myself for not trying to speak to him. Was it really Nick? Was he a member of the Wander Society? Did he leave the newsletters? I can't answer any of these questions with any certainty. But if he is a member, it would have been futile anyway because members don't care to speak about the Wander Society publicly. A conundrum, yes?

That night I sat down with the newspaper and took in every inch of it. It was glorious! An eclectic mix of strange articles, one called "How to Play Tennis," which wasn't at all about playing tennis; "Ode to a Dusty Bookshop" (about taking your time while selecting a book); "How to Choose a Rock"; and "The Mycelium Minute (Six Interesting Facts about Mushrooms)." The inside of the newspaper had a cut-out wheat paste poster of Walt Whitman with instructions for how to make your own wheat paste. The back page had a variety of ads for strange and intriguing things, including a course in cloud contemplation (with no classroom, only self-directed outdoor lessons), and one for a time machine you can make at home, and a Museum of the Unknown—nobody knows what is inside and no one who goes in is allowed to talk about it after they come out. Perhaps most tongue-in-cheek was the top right corner, which read, "Free, when you can find it." That would be the challenge wouldn't it?

Reading it I felt like a kid again, one who had just received a new edition of my favorite childhood magazine that I wanted to savor alone in my room, from cover to cover, over the course of an entire day.

what is your true nature?

TWS awaits.

Solvit^ur

Amb^ulando.

Solvit^ur

Amb^ulando.

Solvit^ur

Amb^ulando.

YOU
HAVE
ARRIVED

YOU
HAVE
ARRIVED

YOU
HAVE
ARRIVED

WE ARE
INFINITE

WE ARE
INFINITE

WE ARE
INFINITE

You must habit yourself to the dazzle
of the light and of every moment of your life.
                                        -WW